NOTES BY NAJOUD ENSAFF

 Long

C333874268

York Press

The right of Najoud Ensaff to be identified as Author of this Work
has been asserted by her in accordance with the Copyright, Designs
and Patents Act 1988

YORK PRESS
322 Old Brompton Road, London SW5 9JH

PEARSON EDUCATION LIMITED
Edinburgh Gate, Harlow,
Essex CM20 2JE, United Kingdom
Associated companies, branches and representatives throughout the world

First published 2006
12

ISBN: 978-1-405-83562-6

Illustrated by Owain Kirby
Typeset by utimestwo, Northamptonshire
Printed in China (CTPS/12)

Contents

Part One
Introduction

How to study a play...5
Author and context 6
Setting and background...8
Character tree..13
Timeline 14

Part Two
Summaries

General summary 16
Detailed summaries
    Act I...19
    Act II 27
    Act III...38

Part Three
Commentary

Themes..49
Structure...54
Characters...56
Language and style...63

Part Four
Resources

How to use quotations...68
Coursework essay...69
Sitting the examination 70
Improve your grade..71
Sample essay plan..75
Further questions...76

Literary terms 77

Checkpoint hints/answers 78

Test answers 81

PREFACE

York Notes are designed to give you a broader perspective on works of literature studied at GCSE and equivalent levels. With examination requirements changing in the twenty-first century, we have made a number of significant changes to this new series. We continue to help students to reach their own interpretation of the text but York Notes now have important extra-value new features.

You will discover that York Notes are genuinely interactive. The new **Checkpoint** features will make sure that you can test your knowledge and broaden your understanding. You will also be directed to excellent websites, books and films where you can follow up ideas for yourself.

The **Resources** section has been updated and an entirely new section has been devoted to how to improve your grade. Careful reading and application of the principles laid out in the Resources section guarantee improved performance.

The **Detailed summaries** include an easy-to-follow skeleton structure of the story-line, while the section on **Language and style** has been extended to offer an in-depth discussion of the writer's techniques.

The Contents page shows the structure of this study guide. However, there is no need to read from the beginning to the end as you would with a novel, play or poem. Use the Notes in the way that suits you. Our aim is to help you with your understanding of the work, not to dictate how you should learn.

Our authors are practising English teachers and examiners who have used their experience to offer a whole range of **Examiner's secrets** – useful hints to encourage exam success.

The author of these Notes is Najoud Ensaff, a former Head of English and Drama and now a GCSE examiner. She has written a variety of educational materials including OCR GCSE English Language Exam Practice Papers, several workbooks and resource packs and, most recently, *The Bell Jar: A Teaching Guide* (2006).

The text used in these Notes is the Heinemann Plays edition, 1993.

PART ONE

INTRODUCTION

HOW TO STUDY A PLAY

Plays are written to be performed, so as well as reading the text, try to see a production, on television, video, DVD or, best of all, on stage. A performance will give you a real sense of what the playwright intended and will bring the play alive for you.

When you study a text, there are certain aspects to look out for:

❶ THE PLOT: a play is a carefully constructed story. Each event that happens has a bearing on the whole play.

❷ THE CHARACTERS: these are the individuals taking part in the 'story' of the play. You will gain an impression of them as the play unfolds. You may find that you like or dislike some, think some are foolish and others noble. The characters may change, or your perceptions of them may alter, during the play.

❸ THE THEMES: these are the ideas in the play, the messages that the playwright wishes you to consider, or the points he or she would like to make e.g., 'life is fragile' or 'ambition can have tragic consequences'.

❹ THE SETTING: this is the time and place that the playwright chooses for the play.

❺ THE LANGUAGE: the writer's choice of words and phrases which are deliberately chosen to help convey characters and ideas.

❻ STAGING AND PERFORMANCE: the type of stage, lighting, scenery, sound effects, acting style and delivery are all considered carefully by the director.

A director has the difficult job of looking at how a playwright has presented the play, and then interpreting it for the stage.

These York Notes will help you to understand what the play is about and will guide you in forming your own interpretation. Do not expect the study of the play to be easy: plays are not written for examination purposes but to be performed!

EXAMINER'S SECRET
Going to see a production may also help you to see the play in a new or interesting way, according to how the director has interpreted it.

EXAMINER'S SECRET
You can come up with a **mnemonic** to help you in an exam. Make up a sentence using the first letters of points one to six to begin each word, e.g. **P**am **C**an **T**ake **S**even **L**ittle **S**teps.

AUTHOR – LIFE AND WORKS	CONTEXT
1896 Robert Cedric Sherriff is born on 6 June in Surrey	
	1901 Queen Victoria dies. Her son becomes King Edward VII
	1905 Germany starts to build warships
1907 Sherriff attends Kingston Grammar School	
	1910 Edward VII dies. His son becomes King George V
1913 He joins the Sun Insurance Office where his father works	
	1914–18 First World War
1915 Sherriff joins the East Surrey Regiment	
	1916 Compulsory military service is introduced in Britain
1917 Sherriff is wounded on active service	
1918 He rejoins Sun Insurance Office as a claims adjudicator	**1918** 11 November: armistice to end the war is signed
1921 Sherriff writes his first play, *The Toilers*	
	1922 Britain gets its first radio station
	1926 General Strike hits British Industry
1928 *Journey's End* is allowed two showings on a Sunday evening and a Monday matinee in December 1929 by the Incorporated Stage Society at the Apollo Theatre. Laurence Olivier is cast as Stanhope	
1929 *Journey's End* opens at the Savoy Theatre on 21 January and runs for two years	**1929** Erich Maria Remarque, who is German, writes *All Quiet on the Western Front*, an anti-war novel

AUTHOR – LIFE AND WORKS

1930 Sherriff and Vernon Bartlett write a book version of *Journey's End*. Sherriff applies to Oxford University

1933 Sherriff writes the screenplay for *The Invisible Man* and *Goodbye Mr Chips*. The latter is nominated for an Oscar

1934 Sherriff leaves Oxford, without completing his degree course. *Two Hearts Doubled* is written

1937 Sherriff donates a scholarship fund to Oxford University

1945 Sherriff writes *Odd Man Out*, which later becomes a film

1955 *The Dam Busters*, for which Sherriff wrote the screenplay, is produced. It is nominated for an award

1968 Sherriff publishes his autobiography *No Leading Lady*

1975 Sherriff dies on 13 November in Kingston Hospital

CONTEXT

1933 Adolph Hitler comes to power as Chancellor of Germany

1939–45 Second World War

1950 Korean War breaks out and involves the British Army

1952 Queen Elizabeth II comes to the throne after the death of her father, George VI

1963 The anti-war play, *Oh What a Lovely War*, is produced in London

1965 Vietnam War starts

1975 Vietnam War ends. Margaret Thatcher becomes Conservative leader in opposition

SETTING AND BACKGROUND

R. C. SHERRIFF'S BACKGROUND

R. C. Sherriff was born on 6 June 1896. Some sources give his place of birth as Kingston-upon-Thames, Surrey, while others record it as Hampton Wick, just across the river in Middlesex. He attended Kingston Grammar School until the age of seventeen. Then he considered applying to Oxford University, but realised that he could not afford it. He did not think that he would get a scholarship, so instead he joined the Sun Insurance Office, where his father and grandfather had previously worked. He remained there until joining the army in 1915 when he was posted to the East Surrey Regiment. He saw active service in France as an infantry soldier until 1917 when he was wounded at Passchendaele. He spent six months in hospital, and then returned to the insurance firm in London.

Sherriff first started writing in order to raise funds for his rowing club in Kingston. He wrote a number of plays, *Journey's End* being his seventh and first successful one. With support from the literary agents Curtis Brown and after a number of rejections from theatre managers, the play was finally given two performances at the Apollo Theatre in London in 1928. It was directed by James Whale and starred Laurence Olivier as Stanhope. In 1929 it opened at the Savoy Theatre in London with Colin Clive in the lead, where it ran for 594 performances, and then 485 perfomances in New York. Sherriff took leave from his insurance post and travelled to America where the play was later made into a film with James Whale again as the director.

In 1930, Sherriff wrote another play called *Badger's Green* but it was not very successful and he started to suspect that he was a one-play man. By now he had bought a large country house in Surrey where he and his mother lived. This house became too expensive for him, so at the age of thirty-four he went to New College, Oxford, to study history in order to become a schoolmaster. When James Whale asked him to write the screenplay for *The Invisible Man* by H. G. Wells he took leave from Oxford to do so, returning in the

DID YOU KNOW?

When Sherriff first tried to get a commission in the army as an officer, he was told that only young men leaving public school were given commissions. The army had to re-think this rule, however, after so many men were killed. In 1915, Sherriff became a captain in the East Surrey Regiment.

CHECK THE BOOK

Sherriff collaborated with Vernon Bartlett and published a novel version of *Journey's End* in 1930. It was less successful than the play.

autumn of 1932. Because of illness, he did not finish his studies at Oxford, and he realised that he was unlikely to get a good degree. Instead, he turned to writing once more, producing twenty-three plays and novels, including *The Four Feathers*, *The Road Back*, *The White Carnation* and *The Siege of Swain Castle*. He died in November 1975.

A FIRST WORLD WAR SETTING

Based on Sherriff's experiences in the war, the play is set in St Quentin, France, in 1918. It starts on Monday 18 March three days before Germany launched 'Operation Michael' – an attack on St Quentin.

Historically accurate, the setting is very important to *Journey's End* as it has come to be viewed as a play about the truth of war. However, Sherriff did not intend the play to explore the rights and wrongs of war. In his autobiography *No Leading Lady*, Sherriff wrote that his characters were 'simple, unquestioning men who fought the war because it seemed the only right and proper thing to do ... (it was a play) in which not a word was spoken against the war ... and no word of condemnation was uttered ....'

In fact, Sherriff believed this was why the play was so successful, as previous and unpopular war plays had carried 'messages' and 'sermons against war'. What Sherriff hoped to do was to show 'how men really lived in the trenches, how they talked and how they behaved' *(No Leading Lady)*. All the same, with Maurice Browne, who was strongly against war, as producer, the play came to be viewed as being anti-war.

First performed in 1928, and published the following year, the play was one of many books, poems and plays about war that were written at that time. When it was first performed no one realised how successful it would be. No one thought that a play about war and with an all male cast would be a hit, but by the end of 1928, *Journey's End* was just that. A theatre critic described it as 'perhaps the greatest of all war plays' *(No Leading Lady)*. It ran for two

 DID YOU KNOW?
When Sherriff died he left his house to Elmbridge Borough Council. The sale of the house, *Rosebriars*, allowed Elmbridge Council to establish a trust to promote the arts.

 CHECK THE NET
The *R. C. Sherriff Trust* still exists today. Find out more at **www. rcsherrifftrust. org.uk**

 DID YOU KNOW?
The 1976 film *Aces High* was based on *Journey's End*, as was the German film *Die Andere Seite* (1930) which presented events from the opposite side.

years, was translated into several languages, and was later performed throughout the world.

STAGING

All the action of the play takes place in the dugout where the British soldiers eat and sleep. Sherriff uses sound and lighting throughout to create a realistic and theatrically effective image of war.

DID YOU KNOW?

As a novice playwright, Sherriff read *Playmaking* by William Archer to help him in his work.

The warren-like nature of dugouts with their entrances and exits lend themselves to the stage. Perhaps more importantly the dugout allows Sherriff to present a real image of life in the trenches, what he calls 'a nostalgic journey into the past' *(No Leading Lady)*.

The importance of the dugout setting is indicated at the start when Hardy is seen drying his sock over a flame and singing about time. The basic living conditions serve as a reminder to the audience of the hardships soldiers went through. They did not know when the war would end, and spent a lot of their time waiting and doing nothing. Their boredom was made worse by the cramped conditions of the trenches. These conditions, however, allowed a closeness between soldiers which Sherriff explores in his play. The fact that even in such conditions, duty, loyalty and bravery emerge demonstrates, as Sherriff intended, the nobility of the soldiers. At the same time, it reminds the audience of the horrible wreckage of their young lives and the futility of their deaths.

SOCIAL AND HISTORICAL CONTEXT

The First World War was a turning point in history. Because of it, the kings and queens in Europe lost most of their power, and the right-wing system of government, known as fascism, took over the government of Italy. The war was one of the reasons why Russia had a revolution and overthrew the Tsar.

CHECK THE NET

Have a look at **www.1914–1918. net** for information on the British army in the First World War.

There is no one thing which led directly to the war. However, the assassination in June 1914 of the Archduke of Austria, Franz Ferdinand, heir to the Austro-Hungarian throne, was probably the starting point. As he had been killed by a man from Serbia, Austria declared war on that country, and, gradually, all the countries in

Europe were drawn into the dispute. The war broke out in August 1914, with Germany on one side and Britain and France on the other. Everyone thought, at first, that it would be a short-lived war, and many young men joined the British Army in search of adventure. They had no idea what the fighting would really be like.

By 1917, America had joined the war, and in 1918 Germany tried one last big attack called the Spring Offensive, in an attempt to break through and separate the British and French forces. At first they had some success but by October 1918 Germany had asked for a ceasefire, and the war came to an end on 11 November 1918. The war had finished but nothing would ever be the same again.

Sherriff wrote *Journey's End* in this post-war era. During the war, people had gone to the theatre to forget their troubles and to be amused. In the 1920s this continued. At the same time, there was a lot of change in the way theatres were managed and, in 1926, talking cinema, i.e. films with audible dialogue, started. The class system was also undergoing massive changes and people who in the past would never have been to the theatre started going. As a result of all of this, commercially successful plays became ones that appealed to the masses. This may explain why few war plays were a success. *Journey's End* was an exception.

In Europe, playwrights and actors reacted against the way the world had changed by experimenting with theatre, but in England few plays were political or commented on social events. Those that did were performed in small independent theatres, mostly outside London. For this reason when Sherriff first took *Journey's End* to London theatres, it was rejected as being potentially unpopular. All the same, it has come to be seen as a very important play.

Although the subject of war was seen as unappealing at the time, Sherriff wrote his play in a traditional form. This helped it to become a success. *Journey's End* proved to be a turning point between old and new theatre. As a result of his total treatment of war, Sherriff opened the way for later playwrights to write about war in a new way. In fact, in the same year, 1928, C. B. Fernald published the play *Tomorrow* and in 1929 Hubert Griffiths' play

 CHECK THE BOOK

All Quiet on the Western Front tells the story of Paul Baumer, a young German soldier serving in the trenches in France in the First World War. It is a book which exposes all the sadness and madness of war.

CHECK THE BOOK

Read *Suspense* by Patrick McGill or Maxwell Anderson's play *What Price Glory?* to see how contemporary playwrights wrote about war.

Tunnel Trench appeared. Both plays treat war in a more symbolic and imaginative way. What Sherriff had managed to do was 'let the war speak' (Carlo Pellizzi and Rowan Williams, *English Drama: the last great phase*).

Now take a break!

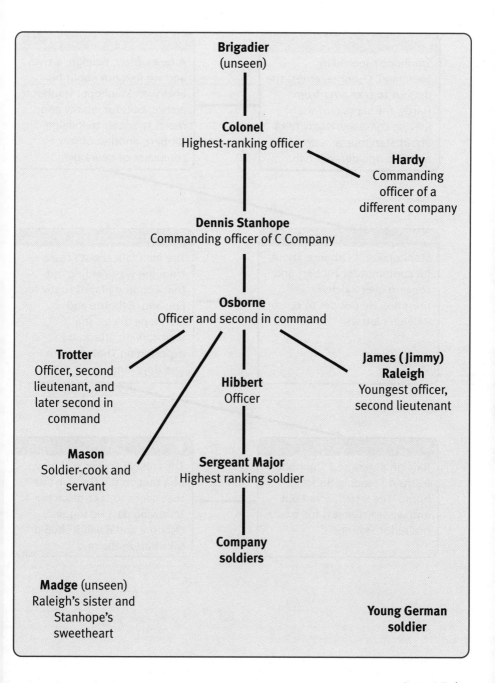

Brigadier
(unseen)

Colonel
Highest-ranking officer

Hardy
Commanding
officer of a
different company

Dennis Stanhope
Commanding officer of C Company

Osborne
Officer and second in command

Trotter
Officer, second
lieutenant, and
later second in
command

Hibbert
Officer

James (Jimmy)
Raleigh
Youngest officer,
second lieutenant

Mason
Soldier-cook and
servant

Sergeant Major
Highest ranking soldier

Company
soldiers

Madge (unseen)
Raleigh's sister and
Stanhope's
sweetheart

Young German
soldier

1

Stanhope's second in command, Osborne, enters the dugout to take over from Hardy, the captain of the leaving company. Hardy talks about Stanhope as a drunkard and Osborne defends him.

2

A new officer, Raleigh, arrives and we find out about his links with Stanhope. Stanhope arrives, calls for whisky and reacts strangely to Raleigh. Hibbert, another officer, complains of neuralgia.

3

Stanhope tells Osborne about his contempt for Hibbert and concern over Raleigh's presence. He decides to censor Raleigh's letters.

4

The men talk about life away from the war. We find out that Osborne played rugby for England. Osborne and Stanhope discuss the forthcoming attack. It is expected on Thursday – in two days' time.

5

Raleigh enters and Stanhope insists on reading his letter home. The letter is read out and we see that it is full of praise for Stanhope.

6

The colonel arrives with news of a raid on the German line that needs to take place the following day. He suggests Osborne and Raleigh should take part in the raid.

7

Hibbert tries to leave but Stanhope threatens to shoot him and then sympathises with him. Hibbert is persuaded to stay and help the others.

8

The officers are told about the raid. Osborne is resigned to his fate, Raleigh is elated and Trotter thinks it is stupid timing.

9

The colonel gives an encouraging talk to the men, promising that Osborne and Raleigh will be awarded a Military Cross for bravery. The raid takes place and Osborne and six others die, but a German soldier is taken prisoner.

10

The German prisoner is interrogated and the colonel seems happy but Raleigh is stunned by his experience and Stanhope is bitter.

11

All the officers eat a celebratory dinner, but Raleigh does not join in. Stanhope sends Hibbert to bed. Trotter is made second in command. When Raleigh appears, he and Stanhope argue.

12

The final German attack comes. Raleigh dies as Stanhope looks after him. Just after Stanhope leaves the stage, the dugout collapses into darkness.

PART TWO

SUMMARIES

DID YOU KNOW?

Sherriff decided upon the name *Journey's End* after reading a line from a book. A chapter in it closed, 'It was late in the evening when we came at last to our Journey's End.' Having considered the names *Suspense* and *Waiting* the playwright felt that *Journey's End* was a more suitable title and chose this instead.

GENERAL SUMMARY

ACT I

It is the evening of Monday 18 March. The play opens in a dugout. Stanhope's company is about to take over from another one. They will be on duty for six days, during which time a German attack is expected. Osborne arrives as Hardy, the other company's commander, is drying his sock and singing. He and Hardy share a drink. They talk about conditions, the present situation and about Stanhope, whom Hardy describes as 'drinking like a fish' (p. 4) and having strained nerves. Osborne defends his commander as dutiful, brave and experienced. He has been at the front for three years. Hardy leaves without waiting to see Stanhope.

A new officer, Raleigh, arrives. It emerges that he knows and admires Stanhope from school and that his sister and Stanhope are close. Osborne tries to warn Raleigh about the changes in Stanhope. He introduces him to the routines of trench life. Mason, the soldier cook, confides in Osborne about a mistake over tinned pineapple so that Stanhope will not blame him. Stanhope appears on stage. He calls for whisky before even seeing Raleigh and when he does notice him he is stunned – 'as though dazed' (p. 18). Trotter, on the other hand, welcomes Raleigh. After eating, Trotter and Raleigh go out on patrol. Hibbert enters the dugout and complains of his neuralgia – a severe pain in his face and head. Stanhope thinks this is just an excuse to get sent home, but Osborne is more sympathetic. The two of them discuss Raleigh and his sister. Stanhope is concerned that Raleigh will betray him in his letters home and decides to censor them. Osborne tries to calm Stanhope; sensing he is tired, he suggests that he goes to bed. Both men turn in for the night.

ACT II

It is the following morning. Stanhope is on duty in the trench and the other officers are enjoying breakfast in the dugout. They talk about Stanhope, who is looking ill, and discuss his strange

GENERAL SUMMARY

behaviour towards Raleigh the previous night. Trotter talks about gardening and nature, then leaves the stage to take over from Stanhope. Raleigh and Osborne talk; it emerges that Osborne was a schoolmaster and had played rugby for Harlequins and England. We gain an impression of Raleigh's views of war before he leaves to finish a letter that he has started to write, just as Stanhope enters the dugout. Stanhope and Osborne discuss the German attack which is expected in two days' time. Stanhope is drinking whisky and is worried about what Raleigh thinks and what he might write in his letter. He is determined to censor it. When Raleigh enters on his way to inspect rifles and puts his letter on the table to be sent, Stanhope tells him to leave it open. After a discussion and struggle, Raleigh is forced to give Stanhope the letter and leaves. Stanhope is too ashamed to look at it and eventually Osborne reads it. Unexpectedly, it is full of praise for Stanhope.

That afternoon, Stanhope issues details of work to a sergeant major which he wants carried out before the German attack. The colonel arrives and instructs Stanhope that he is to organise a raiding party for the following day. He suggests that Osborne and (despite Stanhope's objections) Raleigh lead the party. Stanhope is to have supper with the colonel and the colonel will talk to Osborne and Raleigh the following morning.

Hibbert enters the dugout, having been asleep. He complains about his neuralgia and asks to go down the line and seek medical help. Stanhope refuses and threatens to shoot him 'by accident' (p. 56) if he tries to leave. Eventually Stanhope confides in Hibbert that he too is scared and encourages him to stay to help the others. Hibbert says he will try.

Osborne returns to the dugout and is told of the raid by Stanhope. He is soon followed by Trotter who is also informed of the raid which he feels is badly timed. He asks what Osborne is reading. It is *Alice's Adventures in Wonderland*. Stanhope and Hibbert leave to relieve Raleigh, and Osborne writes a letter. Raleigh returns to the dugout and seems to be excited at the thought of going on a raid.

EXAMINER'S SECRET

Look at *what* happens and *when*. Often a playwright will precede and follow a tense moment with some light relief.

CHECK THE BOOK

Read some poetry by Wilfred Owen or Siegfried Sassoon, two soldier poets, to complement your studies of the play. You could look at *Spring Offensive, Dulce et Decorum Est* and *Strange Meeting* by Owen and *Does it Matter?* and *Attack* by Sassoon.

ACT III

It is Wednesday afternoon. The colonel has arrived with last-minute instructions and words of encouragement for the raiding party. Osborne and Raleigh sit for a few minutes before the raid. They talk about home and trivial things. Osborne puts his wedding ring on the table and the two of them leave for the raid. Noises of gunfire and shells are heard offstage. Stanhope and the colonel appear on stage with the captured German soldier who Stanhope leaves the colonel to question. He returns and rather bitterly tells the colonel that Osborne and six men have been killed. Raleigh enters and is congratulated by the colonel, but is unable to speak. Stanhope comments that Raleigh is sitting on Osborne's bed.

That evening, Trotter, Hibbert and Stanhope share stories and jokes about women, having eaten together. Raleigh has not eaten with them but has remained on duty in the trench. Hibbert and Stanhope argue and Hibbert is sent to bed. Trotter is made second in command then goes to relieve Raleigh. Stanhope is angry that Raleigh did not eat with the officers. The two argue and Raleigh expresses his confusion over Stanhope's attitude to Osborne's death. Stanhope makes it clear that he uses drink to help him cope. Raleigh tries to apologise but is told to leave and they part on bad terms.

The following morning the officers wake. The sound of German shells is heard, signalling the attack. Trotter and Raleigh go out to the front line. Hibbert holds back, but eventually he and Mason leave.

Stanhope is told that Raleigh has been hurt, so he has him brought into the dugout where it becomes clear that, although Raleigh does not know it himself, his wounds are serious. Stanhope comforts Raleigh and gives him water, but he dies. Stanhope leaves the dugout as the sound of shelling rises. *There is darkness in the dugout* and *'the red dawn glows'* (p. 103). The play ends as the *'dull rattle of machine guns'* (p. 103) is heard: we may assume that the whole company have met with their deaths.

DID YOU KNOW?

Winston Churchill, who was then Chancellor of the Exchequer, was a fan of the play. He wrote to Sherriff full of praise for *Journey's End* and in his letter asked him to explain a few questions relating to the end scene. He and Sherriff later met at Downing Street.

Detailed summaries

PART ONE (PP. 1–8) – Osborne takes over from Hardy

1 Hardy is drying his sock and singing when Osborne arrives.

2 He and Osborne discuss trench conditions and Hardy explains the present situation, referring to a map.

3 They talk about Stanhope's reputation and drinking.

4 Hardy leaves without seeing Stanhope.

These opening pages set the scene for the audience, providing them with information about the conditions of war and its effect on men. We also gain insights into characters.

The stage directions describe the starkness of the setting where candles light the *'dugout'* (p. 1) and only whisky, water and a mug sit on a table. The chaos and untidiness are shown through words such as *'litter of papers'* (p. 1) and *'jumbled mass'* (p. 1). It is clear that disinfectant is added to drinking water to kill microbes and this is an early indication of the sort of conditions soldiers suffer. The floor is damp, and rats and earwigs are later mentioned. All these help to establish the setting as an unwelcome environment where earwig races provide an evening's entertainment.

Hardy's physical description contrasts with Osborne's and suggests their differing personalities. Hardy is cheerful, seen here singing. He is flippant and clearly untidy and disorganised, leaving many of the details to the sergeant major, while Osborne is 'fussy' (p. 4) and keen to get everything prepared correctly for Stanhope. Hardy even leaves before Stanhope arrives, aware of his comparatively low standards.

Hardy's song is clearly intended to relieve his boredom but his words are telling. He sings of women in a place where there are none and he refers to time, 'Tick! — Tock!— wind up the clock, and we'll start the day over again' (p. 1). For the soldiers in the trenches, life is a waiting game. 'Sometimes nothing happens for hours on end; then — all of a sudden — "over she comes!" — rifle grenades

CHECKPOINT 3

What information does Hardy pass on to Osborne about the front line and trench stores?

—Minnies — and those horrid little things like pineapples — you know' (p. 2).

He provides the audience with information about the expected German attack and details of guns and 'posts' (p. 3). We learn through his conversations with Osborne that Stanhope's company are expecting a new officer to arrive soon.

> **Hardy's view on Stanhope**
>
> Hardy describes Stanhope as a 'freak' (p. 5), a hardened drinker, and implies that Osborne would make a better commander. Through his conversations with Osborne, we learn that Stanhope has not gone home on leave and has been commanding the company for three years straight from school.
>
> As the play proceeds the audience will gain greater insight into Stanhope through what others say and do and through what we see of Stanhope himself. See if your views of Stanhope change as the play progresses.

PART TWO (PP. 9–17) – OSBORNE AND RALEIGH TALK

CHECKPOINT 4

What does Osborne do to help Raleigh settle in?

1. Mason lays the table for supper and he and Osborne discuss the food.
2. The new officer, Raleigh, arrives.
3. He and Osborne talk about his connection with Stanhope.
4. Osborne introduces Raleigh to trench life.
5. Mason meets Raleigh and explains the mix-up over the tinned pineapple to Osborne, then leaves to dish out the soup.

We gain insights into various characters in this section of the play.

Osborne's approachable and easy way with the soldiers is evident in his light-hearted discussion with Mason and later Raleigh. He is the one in whom Mason confides over the mistake over the tinned pineapple. Osborne tells Raleigh that the others call him 'uncle' (p. 10), suggesting that the younger soldiers go to him for advice. He tells Raleigh to wait for the others before unpacking and introduces him to trench life. He and Raleigh discuss the fact that it is quiet, which highlights the terrible feeling that something is about to happen. This waiting was part of trench life, but few soldiers expected it. Raleigh is surprised, 'I never thought it was like that' (p. 15). This shows his inexperience, and also indicates the false expectations many had of war.

Sherriff uses Raleigh to represent the romantic, idealistic beginner: his *'boyish voice'* is contrasted with a *'gruff (and we may assume more experienced) voice'* (p. 9) from the start. He is seen to be nervous and impressionable. His hesitant speech and Sherriff's directions, *'self-consciously'*, *'laughs nervously'* (p. 10), suggest a young and inexperienced officer.

With the entrance of Raleigh, we learn more about Stanhope, who has not yet appeared. Raleigh's determination to join Stanhope's company shows that the latter is a person who commands loyalty, a different image from that presented by Hardy at the start of the play. Raleigh's view of Stanhope is that of a man untouched by war, someone with a past and with a sweetheart, a man at his best. His reference to Stanhope's anger at boys drinking whisky is ironic in light of what we have already heard of Stanhope's drinking. We realise this as Osborne tells us and Raleigh that he 'mustn't expect to find him – quite the same' (p. 13). War has changed him: it has been 'a big strain' (p. 13) on him.

The language that the two men use and their topic of conversation – rugby and cricket – remind us of their public school background, and of life away from war – as Osborne says, 'a long way from here' (p. 11) . The talk of food adds comic relief: Osborne's mock shock at Mason's mixed tinned fruit story, 'Good heavens! It must have given you a turn' (p. 16), helps to lighten the waiting game of trench life. For these men of the First World War, these diversions from their immediate surroundings are essential to their survival.

> **CHECKPOINT 5**
>
> During the play, what diversions do the men find here and elsewhere?

> **GLOSSARY**
>
> **Minnies** German guns, minethrowers
>
> **post** place where a soldier stands guard

PART THREE (PP. 17–23) – THE ARRIVAL OF STANHOPE

1 Stanhope and Trotter enter the dugout.

2 Stanhope reacts to Raleigh's arrival.

3 Food is served.

4 Trotter and Raleigh go on patrol.

CHECKPOINT 6

How does Stanhope's behaviour show us he is startled and unhappy to see Raleigh?

CHECKPOINT 7

How is Trotter's fascination with food made evident to us and what do you think is its purpose?

We gain our first glimpse of Stanhope here. Sherriff's stage directions establish him as young and good-looking with a smart uniform, yet the *'pallor under his skin and dark shadows under his eyes'* (p. 17) indicate the strain he has been under. He is slim in sharp contrast with the *'short and fat'* (p. 17) Trotter. His character, too, is very different from Trotter's.

Stanhope's concern over cleanliness and tidiness is evident in his *'carefully brushed'* hair, his *'well-cut and cared for'* uniform and in his reaction to the 'mess' (p. 17) the trenches have been left in. His first call is for whisky, not soup, showing that what Hardy had said of him is true. At seeing Raleigh, Stanhope's initial confidence is replaced with stunned *'silence'* and a low voiced remark of 'How did you — get here?' (p. 18). He has been caught off-guard and the tension in the dugout is clear. Osborne's and then Trotter's failed efforts to relieve this by referring to the mix-up over pineapple chunks are brushed aside by Stanhope who is concentrating on Raleigh. He is clearly affected by his presence and self-consciously puts on a show of '*gaiety*' (p. 18) as he sits to eat. Even Trotter notices the change in his 'skipper', telling him to 'cheer up' (p. 21). However, they cannot change Stanhope's mood. He tells Mason off about the lack of pepper in the soup, threatening him with removal and he orders a soldier to borrow some from another company.

Trotter's character is firmly established as different from the other officers. Unlike them he talks with a working-class accent and has clearly not been to public school. However, his carefree and jovial attitude to life helps to lighten the atmosphere.

Trotter evidently likes his food; we may feel that he uses it in the same way as Stanhope uses drink. Osborne comically refers to this when he says, 'That's because you never stop eating' (p. 22). Trotter warmly welcomes Raleigh after Stanhope has been unfriendly; his relaxed conversation with him and the comic play over the boxes used for seats lighten the mood, as does the talk about food.

Trotter's response to the boredom of trench life is to draw 'a hundred and forty-four' circles, each representing an hour, which he will black in to make 'time go all right' (p. 22). This and his flippant remark that revolvers are needed to shoot rats make clear that he is someone who has found ways to cope with stress.

We are reminded again of conditions in the trenches when Osborne refers to the need for pepper as a disinfectant and when Trotter talks of rats. During Trotter and Osborne's discussion about war, it becomes apparent that, alongside the quiet, the men have to put up with not knowing what will happen next – 'I wish we knew more of what's going on' (p. 20). Yet Trotter, who is able to make light of the situation, helps Raleigh to go on patrol with a sense of optimism.

 DID YOU KNOW?

Sherriff kept a diary while he was in the trenches and in it he recounted someone complaining of French shops having 'nothink but tinned apricots and lime juice'.

GLOSSARY

skipper slang meaning captain

PART FOUR (PP. 23–31) – STANHOPE AND OSBORNE TALK

3 Stanhope talks to Osborne about Hibbert.

4 The conversation turns to Raleigh and his sister.

5 Stanhope worries that his drinking will be revealed. He decides to censor Raleigh's letters.

6 He and Osborne turn in for the night.

DID YOU KNOW?

'No-man's-land' was the land between German and British frontline trenches. It was sometimes only a few feet wide.

Hibbert's entrance introduces us to the conflict in the play between cowardice and heroism. We see the psychological effects of war on a man. Hibbert is viewed unsympathetically by Stanhope who thinks he is using 'neuralgia' (p. 24) as an excuse to leave the front. He calls him a 'worm' (p. 25) and resents his desire to go home and spend the rest of the war in comfort, leaving everyone else to suffer.

CHECKPOINT 8

Do you think Stanhope is right to view Hibbert as a 'worm'?

When they talk it is clear that Osborne is a friend and support to Stanhope. Osborne can see the utter exhaustion in Stanhope. He says that the colonel recognises that leave is 'due to' (p. 27) him, but Stanhope is resistant to the idea. He feels it is an easy way out, although he admits he is worried that his luck might be coming to an end. He also shows his unhappiness over his changed image by revealing to Osborne his fears, 'without being doped with whisky – I'd go mad with fright' (p. 27). We learn that it was the horrors he saw at the battle of Vimy Ridge, a real event, which caused Stanhope to take to drink. We also see that he is very worried that Raleigh might reveal the truth of his changed character to his sister. Despite Osborne's encouraging Stanhope to look favourably at Raleigh and view his hero-worship as a compliment, and despite his words of reassurance, Stanhope continues to look at things in a 'rather black sort of way' (p. 28). He clearly feels responsible for Raleigh and is torn between his desire to protect him and his selfish need to prevent the truth from reaching Madge.

CHECKPOINT 9

What do we learn about Stanhope and his relationship with Raleigh's sister?

When Osborne tucks Stanhope into bed despite his quarrelsome behaviour, we see Osborne once more taking on the role of carer. The closeness between the two officers makes Stanhope's later loss all the greater. Symbolically at the end of Act I, Osborne winds up his watch, as if suggesting to us that the move towards an end is only a matter of time.

CHECKPOINT 10

Where else does Stanhope use his power in an abusive way?

Stanhope's state of mind

Stanhope's distressed state is clear from his frenzied and insistent words, 'He's a little prig. Wants to write home and tell Madge all about me. Well, he won't; d'you see, Uncle? He won't write' (p. 29). His decision to censor Raleigh's letters is a sign of the despair and paranoia he feels. It is an example of the abuse of power that we see Stanhope demonstrate on a number of occasions in the play.

GLOSSARY

neuralgia pain in the face and head associated with injury to nerves

worm a person who is nasty or unethical and does not deserve respect

Now take a break!

WHO SAYS ...?

1 'It's — it's not exactly what I thought. It's just this — this quiet that seems so funny'

....

2 'You see, sir, I know the captain can't stand the sight of apricots. 'E said next time we 'ad them 'e'd wring my neck'

....

4 'You've done longer out here than any man in the battalion. It's time you went away for a rest'

....

3 '... war's bad enough with pepper — but war without pepper — '

....

ABOUT WHOM?

5 'You *are* a fussy old man. Anybody'd think you were in the army'

....

6 'You see, he's been out here a long time. It — it tells on a man — rather badly —

....

8 'He's not a damned little swine who'd deceive his sister'

....

7 'I don't see how you can prevent a fellow going sick'

....

Check your answers on p. 81.

PART ONE (PP. 32–6) – OSBORNE AND TROTTER TALK ABOUT GARDENING

1 The men eat breakfast; Stanhope is on duty and therefore absent.

2 The men discuss Stanhope.

3 Osborne and Trotter share memories of gardening.

4 Trotter leaves to go on duty.

As in other sections of the play, Sherriff uses food as light relief after the tension of the last act and Stanhope's decision to censor Raleigh's letters. Trotter's love of eating is once more evident and serves as a source of comedy.

The fact that a bird sounds funny to Trotter is significant: it is as if Sherriff is saying that men at war feel separated from the real world. Normal rules of nature no longer apply. This is made even more obvious when Trotter tells his story about the may-tree mix-up. The constant references to quiet are a reminder that the attack is imminent and suggest to the audience the coming tragedy. The talk of duties and war as well as jam makes us acutely aware how war has become the normal state of affairs for these men.

> **DID YOU KNOW?**
> British forces at the Western Front had to carry about thirty kilos of equipment, including ammunition, clothing, toiletries, rations and message book.

CHECKPOINT 11

List as many references to quiet as you can find from this section of the play. What is their significance?

CHECK THE BOOK
Sebastian Faulks' novel *Birdsong* was published in 1993. It follows the experiences of Stephen Wraysford and tells the story of soldiers in the First World War.

CHECKPOINT 12

How do you think Raleigh is feeling and why?

When Stanhope's character is discussed his strong sense of duty is made clear. Trotter says 'Nobody'd be well who went on like he does' (p. 34). His service to his country is recognised by his company and he is respected for this. However, his men are not unaware of the effects of such service on their commander. They see as we do that he is 'ill' and that his behaviour is erratic. His telling Raleigh to go to bed 'just as if Raleigh'd been a school kid' (p. 35) seems strange to Trotter. However, it is a reminder to us that they had known each other before the war and of Stanhope's desire to protect Raleigh as he once did at school.

When the conversation moves to gardening we see how sharing memories of home comforts the two older and married officers, Osborne and Trotter.

PART TWO (PP. 37–40) – OSBORNE AND RALEIGH TALK ABOUT RUGBY

1 **Raleigh gives his first impressions of the front.**

2 **Raleigh gets to know Osborne.**

3 **Raleigh goes to write a letter, as Stanhope enters the dugout.**

Osborne is once more presented as a man the other soldiers find approachable. He and Raleigh discuss Raleigh's first impressions of war, and the grinding effect of boredom is again made clear, 'I feel I've been here ages' (p. 37). Raleigh and Osborne's conversation also draws attention to the divide between the men at the front and the politicians whose war they are fighting. In typical public school language, Raleigh says, 'The Germans are really quite decent, aren't they?' (p. 39). Osborne tells a story which suggests the humanity that exists on both sides – 'A big German officer ... called out, "Carry him!"... and ... fired some lights for them to see by' (p. 39). Sherriff demonstrates the futility of war when Osborne goes on to describe how, despite the enemy soldier's compassion, 'Next day we blew each other's trenches to blazes' (p. 39) and just like Raleigh we recognise how 'silly' it all seems.

CHECKPOINT 13

What parallels can you see between rugby and war?

The talk of rugby symbolises the life these men had outside of war where the only games they played were not those of politicians but sport. Raleigh's inexperience is seen again when he suggests that Osborne's having played for England should be shared with the others. Unlike Raleigh, Osborne recognises that 'It doesn't make much difference out here!'(p. 38). The 'natural' (p. 39) rules, which Raleigh longs for, no longer apply.

Dramatic irony is clear when Raleigh refers to writing a letter just as Stanhope enters. We are reminded of the latter's desire to censor material and we expect some sort of quarrel.

An unnatural world

War comes to replace the normal. Sherriff presents the unreality of war in a realistic way. Throughout the play he shows how men are forced to endure a world which is 'frightfully quiet and uncanny' (p. 37), where natural laws dissolve, and time takes on a new dimension, '— and yet I've only been here twelve hours' (p. 37). This is a world where men are left yearning to 'sit and read under trees' (p. 37) and only some are able to keep things in 'proportion' (p. 37).

PART THREE (PP. 40–5) – NEWS OF THE ATTACK AND TALK OF WAR

1. **Stanhope gives Raleigh his orders and talks to Osborne about the need to strengthen the company's defences.**

2. **They talk about the attack and the colonel's news.**

3. **They discuss Trotter and imagination.**

4. **Stanhope talks about his feelings.**

5. **Focus again turns to Raleigh and his letter.**

Stanhope's abilities as a leader and strategist are seen here when he talks to Osborne about the company's 'strong position' (p. 41) and the need to protect themselves. The imminence of the German attack is made clear. The news that the attack will happen whilst C Company is on duty is followed by Osborne's understated 'Oh well'

 DID YOU KNOW?

On Christmas morning of 1914, an unofficial truce broke out between German and British soldiers in the trenches. The two sides entered 'no-man's-land', played a friendly football match and exchanged gifts.

CHECKPOINT 14

Why does Osborne say, 'Tuppence to talk to me now!' (p. 38)?

CHECKPOINT 15

Find examples of humour in this section of the play.

GLOSSARY

blazes hell or hellfire

(p. 41) which shows clearly the tension in the silence which follows Stanhope's announcement. The news is further worsened by the fact that the company will be left alone in the attack without 'any help from behind' (p. 41). When Osborne finally says, 'Well, I'm glad it's coming at last. I'm sick of waiting' (p. 41), we are again reminded of the torturous effect of time, something that Stanhope is clearly affected by – 'thousands of Germans, waiting and thinking' (p. 43).

His reaction to Trotter's chart is telling; it is as if Stanhope envies Trotter's lack of imagination because he believes it keeps him sane. Stanhope's discussion about worms and seeing through things demonstrates his frailty and recognition of his coming end. His suggestion that he struggles 'to get back — and can't' (p. 43) leads us and Osborne to believe that his mind is affected, although Osborne reassures Stanhope that it's just a 'bit of nerve strain' (p. 43). Despite this, Stanhope, himself, recognises the possibility that he might be 'going potty' (p. 43), revealing his state of mind.

Mason's entrance relieves the tension and conversation moves to thoughts of home before Stanhope once again turns to Raleigh and censorship. Despite Osborne's reassurances Stanhope is desperately concerned that Raleigh will tell his sister about Stanhope's drinking in his letter home.

CHECK THE NET

Research the role women played in the Great War. Go to **www.bbc.co.uk** and enter 'First World War' into the search engine. From the World War One homepage you should find links to various articles on women.

CHECKPOINT 16

Why do you think Stanhope and Osborne talk about worms?

CHECKPOINT 17

Do you think Stanhope is justified in wishing to censor Raleigh's letter?

PART FOUR (PP. 45–8) – THE LETTER IS REVEALED

1. **Raleigh enters to silence.**

2. **Stanhope demands to see the letter and Raleigh gives in.**

3. **Stanhope is ashamed and Osborne reads the letter.**

On Raleigh's entrance he becomes aware of the silence, and it is Osborne who seeks to reassure him, trying to relieve the tension in the dugout. However, when Raleigh asks where to leave his letter, Stanhope interrupts in a quiet, and we may presume ominous, voice, 'You leave it open' (p .46). Despite Raleigh's protests, Stanhope bullies him to the point that he is left staring *wide-eyed at Stanhope who is trembling and breathing heavily*' (p. 46).

Raleigh's embarrassment and nervousness gain sympathy from the audience who are aware of Stanhope's state of mind and now see his uncontrollable behaviour. Raleigh's understated 'Right' (p. 46) and quiet exit, as well as Osborne's exclamation at Stanhope, portray Raleigh as the innocent victim in this conflict. Stanhope remains firm for only a moment before sinking down at the table and throwing the letter on to it. He is embarrassed at his behaviour, exclaiming 'Oh God! I don't want to read the blasted thing!' (p. 47). It is Osborne who once again tries to calm the situation, offering to read the letter for him.

The Moment of Truth

Sherriff has built us up to believe that Raleigh will have told his sister about Stanhope being a drunkard so that when we hear, as Stanhope does, of his admiration and praise for him we are filled with regret. We recognise the bitter irony of events. It is this that causes the stunned silence on stage and Stanhope's murmuring and heavy movements. He is ashamed at his underestimation of Raleigh, and moves into the shadows on the stage. We see, as Stanhope does, that Raleigh is clearly more aware of his captain's worth than Stanhope believed. The shining sun at the end of this scene is symbolic of the light of knowledge that the letter brings for all of us.

> **CHECKPOINT 18**
>
> How does Sherriff make us believe that Raleigh has written something incriminating in his letter?

> **CHECKPOINT 19**
>
> Look at Stanhope's actions on p. 47. How do they suggest that he is nervous about the letter's contents?

> **GLOSSARY**
> **potty** mad

PART FIVE (PP. 48–53) – TACTICS AND NEWS OF A RAID

❶ Stanhope explains that the attack is expected on Thursday and the company is to stand firm and not retreat.

❷ The colonel arrives and tells Stanhope about the proposed raid.

❸ Osborne and Raleigh are to lead the raid.

When Stanhope talks to the sergeant major, we see him in his role as commanding officer. It is clear from the conversation that the situation is hopeless and that Stanhope is acting under orders. To the sergeant major's question, 'but what 'appens when the Boche 'as all got round the back of us?' (p. 50) all Stanhope can do is adopt a patriotic stance, saying that the company should 'advance and win the war' (p. 50). He adds the explanation 'If you're told to stick where you are you don't make plans to retire' (p. 50).

With the entrance of the colonel comes confirmation of the date for the big German attack, a sure sign that there is no escape for the men. Alongside this comes news that before this a British raid is to take place on the German line. It will be in daytime under a smoke-screen cover. Both the colonel and Stanhope think the timing is wrong, but the general, who is not present, has given his orders and, just as Stanhope must follow his orders, so the colonel must follow the general's.

Stanhope's bravery is made clear when he offers to lead the raid himself; however, his importance as commander means that the colonel dismisses this idea. In response to the colonel's suggestion of Raleigh for the raid, Stanhope says, 'It's rotten to send a fellow who's just arrived' (p. 53), showing the responsibility he still feels towards his old school friend. Despite the colonel's assurances that the raid is necessary, all Stanhope can manage is a resigned utterance of 'I suppose it is' (p. 53).

In trying to comfort Stanhope the colonel reminds him of the dinner he is invited to, at which he will have fish, a rare treat in wartime. The colonel leaves, promising to return the next morning to speak to the men.

CHECKPOINT 20

Who is to defend left and right flanks of the trenches?

CHECKPOINT 21

What is the purpose of the raid?

Whether Sherriff intended us to read these events as criticisms of the way absent politicians and high-ranking soldiers sent men to their deaths is not certain, but what can be concluded is that in any war the possibility of being killed is real and for C Company time is fast running out.

PART SIX (PP. 54–8) – STANHOPE CONFRONTS HIBBERT

1 Hibbert tries to get sick leave.

2 Stanhope threatens to shoot him.

3 Hibbert stands his ground and Stanhope changes his approach.

4 Hibbert agrees to stay.

With thoughts of the impending raid and attack, Stanhope's mood is irritable, so that when Hibbert enters to discuss his neuralgia, we are aware of the possibility of conflict. Earlier in the play Stanhope had made clear his views on Hibbert and his supposed illness. When Hibbert enters the scene he does not know this but we, the audience, do. The dramatic irony of this and the fact that Stanhope is already unhappy because of the upcoming raid leaves us expecting a conflict. We know that Stanhope is unlikely to view Hibbert, or any of his requests, favourably.

Stanhope has talked to the doctor, as he said he would, so Hibbert cannot now go and see him. However, Stanhope's complete lack of sympathy in the face of Hibbert's fear may lead some to question his tactics. His silent threat to shoot Hibbert as *'He takes out his revolver and stands casually examining it'* (p. 55) and his later spoken threat may cause the audience to be less sympathetic to him. However, his ability to win Hibbert round in the end is a testament to his qualities as a leader. When Stanhope's tough approach is unsuccessful and Hibbert strikes *'blindly at Stanhope'* (p. 55) then dares him to shoot, Stanhope recognises the desperation in Hibbert. He adopts a different tactic, confiding in him in a way we have previously only seen him confide in Osborne –'We *all* feel like you do sometimes, if you only knew. I hate and loathe it all' (p. 57). He makes Hibbert feel he is not alone, even offering to 'see if we can stick it together' (p. 57). He plays on Hibbert's feelings of guilt, his

CHECKPOINT 22

How is tension created in this section of the play?

GLOSSARY
Boche Germans

DID YOU KNOW?

During the First World War, execution for desertion was intended both as punishment and a deterrent to others.

loyalty to the other men and his sense of duty, honour and decency so that in the end Hibbert agrees that he'll try.

The endless waiting

This is our first real insight into Hibbert who has been described by Stanhope as a 'worm' (p. 25) and 'shirker' (p. 55). His complete despair is shown in his hysterical outbursts that he is going mad with the pain, is going to die and then his complete disregard for his life when Stanhope threatens to shoot him. Sherriff presents us with an image of a man who has been psychologically damaged by war. He would prefer to know when he is going to die and be 'ready' (p. 56) for it rather than face the endless waiting, not knowing when or how his death will come, and believing that 'every sound' (p. 57) could be his last.

PART SEVEN (PP. 59–65) – THE RAID IS DISCUSSED

1 Tea and bread are served.

2 Stanhope tells Osborne about the raid, then leaves to ask for volunteers.

3 Trotter enters the dugout and he and Osborne talk.

4 Raleigh enters, excited at having been chosen for the raid.

The tension of the last scene is at first relieved by the discussion over food and the onion tea. When Osborne enters and talk turns to the raid, the scene once more becomes tense. The men's pauses and stilted conversation with Osborne's 'Oh' (p. 60) and repeated 'I see' (p. 60) demonstrate the latter's shock and recognition of danger. Stanhope's apology, 'I'm damn sorry' (p. 60) makes clear to us that he knows that the raid will not be without its casualties. However the fact that Osborne accepts the situation and knows that Stanhope will be able to recruit volunteers for the raid shows the heroism of the company and the loyalty Stanhope commands.

When Trotter and Osborne talk about the raid, we are once more reminded of the distance between the soldiers at war and those who make decisions regarding events at the front. Osborne's controlled and understated treatment of the subject highlights the way in which people's lives are being treated as unimportant. Only Trotter openly states how stupid it all seems, 'Joking apart. It's damn ridiculous making a raid when the Boche are expecting it' (p. 63). Yet Osborne's control will be of benefit to the impressionable Raleigh. As Raleigh enters the dugout, Osborne warns Trotter not to worry him.

It is significant that at such a moment of crisis Osborne should look for an escape by reading *Alice in Wonderland*. However, despite the apparent pointlessness of the rhyme about the crocodile, it holds a truth. Like the crocodile who charms and smiles, the First World War enticed men to join up in the hope of glory, only for them to be used as cannon fodder:

CHECK THE BOOK

Why not read *Private Peaceful*? It's a novel set during the First World War, and written by the former Children's Laureate, Michael Morpurgo.

CHECKPOINT 23

What preparation for the raid will be made overnight?

CHECKPOINT 24

How does Trotter show his concern for Stanhope and why does Stanhope reject his idea?

'How cheerfully he seems to grin
And neatly spreads his claws,
And welcomes little fishes in
With gently smiling jaws!' (p. 64)

CHECKPOINT 25

How is Trotter's
curiosity about
Hibbert made
clear?

The scene and act end with lasting images of war – Osborne writing what will be his last letter to his wife, Stanhope going on duty with a terrified Hibbert, and Raleigh returning from duty with all the excitement of a new recruit hungry for glory and unaware of its cost.

 **CHECK
THE NET**
You can find out
more about Lewis
Carroll by going to
**www.lewiscarroll
society.org.uk**

 Now take a break!

WHO SAYS ...?

1 'I made a rockery when I was home on leave'

....

2 'At the end of the forty-fifth circle I'm going to draw a picture of Trotter being blown up in four pieces'

....

4 'Stanhope — if you only *knew* how awful I feel — Please do let me go by —'

....

3 'But it's — it's private. I didn't know —'

....

ABOUT WHOM?

5 'My goodness, Uncle, doesn't he look ill!'

....

6 'One thing a boy like that can't stand is a smell that isn't fresh'

....

8 'Were you and I picked — specially?'

....

7 'If you ask me, 'e's been crying'

....

Check your answers on p. 81.

PART ONE (PP. 66–9) – THE COLONEL GIVES HIS PEP TALK

1 Stanhope and the colonel discuss last-minute arrangements.

2 The colonel talks to Osborne and Raleigh and then goes with Stanhope to talk to the men.

Stanhope's nervousness is apparent in his pacing and his anxious look at his watch, indicating the importance of time. It is clear that he had hoped for a change of plans when he talks to the colonel, ' … didn't you suggest we altered our plans and made a surprise raid farther up the line after dark?' (p. 66). The reason given for the fast pace of events sounds feeble and Stanhope's bitter comment, 'They can't have it later because of dinner, I suppose' (p. 67) shows how unhappy he is with his commanding officers' decisions. Despite the colonel's insistence that he can't disobey orders, Stanhope makes another suggestion which is dismissed, before he finally resigns himself to events.

It is clear that circumstances are difficult given the red rags which the enemy has placed along the wire, suggesting the men's deaths. Yet Stanhope is able to boost morale and reports that the men 'take it as a joke' (p. 68). The colonel's attempts at encouragement sound weak. It is clear that he feels uncomfortable about the

EXAMINER'S SECRET

Make sure you understand the wording of a question. Words like *examine*, *evaluate*, *analyse* and *explore* often come up, so be clear about what is being asked.

situation as stage directions indicate him lingering, then *'an awkward pause. Then the colonel clears his throat and speaks'* (p. 69). His offer of a Military Cross to Osborne and Raleigh is received with murmured thanks and his last encouraging words that their actions could win the war are forgotten when he reminds them to empty their pockets. By this he means that they might be taken prisoner and they should remove anything that might be of use to the enemy.

PART TWO (PP. 69–76) – THE MEN BEFORE THE RAID

❶ Osborne gives his personal belongings to Stanhope.

❷ Osborne and Raleigh talk over the raid.

❸ They talk about home.

❹ Sounds offstage indicate the raid.

Osborne, an experienced officer, recognises the dangers of the raid and, in preparation for the possibility of being killed, he passes on his belongings to Stanhope. For the audience this signals the coming tragedy. His awkward laugh and Stanhope's pauses and later laughter suggest the tension of the scene, where Stanhope's words, 'You're coming back, old man!' (p. 70) sound hollow.

The awkwardness is increased when Raleigh and Osborne wait for the raid. They smoke and talk, Osborne trying to encourage Raleigh with thoughts of celebration and rum. The silences and pauses once more indicate the fear and tension on stage. Their last minute discussion of the raid provides some reassurance but in an effort to lighten the mood Osborne recites a rhyme from *Alice in Wonderland,* and discussions turn to thoughts of home. Raleigh's repeated invitations to Osborne to visit 'one day' (p. 73) are **ironic** given later events.

After this momentary relief of tension, Osborne looks at his watch, signalling the return to reality. Discussions again centre on the raid and celebrations afterwards. When Raleigh notices Osborne's ring on the table, the latter is not entirely truthful about his reasons for leaving it. We are once more shown Osborne in his role as carer and

 CHECK THE NET

You can read real accounts of individual experiences of the First World War in the Human Face of War section of the BBC site dedicated to the Great War. Go to **www.bbc.co.uk** and enter 'First World War' into the search engine to find the World War One homepage.

CHECKPOINT 26

Where does Osborne admit to Raleigh his true feelings?

GLOSSARY

line Front line

supporter; here he is seen protecting Raleigh from the knowledge of his true motives. The pauses and nervous laughter again suggest anxiety as the men leave for the raid.

This is shortly followed by sounds of rockets and guns rising to *'confused turmoil'* (p. 76) and a *'shriek and a crash'* (p. 76) before dying down as voices are heard in the trench outside.

PART THREE (PP. 76–80) – AFTER THE RAID

1. **Stanhope and the colonel enter.**
2. **Sergeant major brings the German captive on stage.**
3. **The colonel questions him.**
4. **Stanhope reports the deaths to the colonel.**
5. **Raleigh enters, is congratulated by the colonel and sits on Osborne's bed before moving at Stanhope's insistence.**

The chaos of events is evident as a shell crashes nearby just as the colonel and Stanhope enter the dugout. When the young German boy is questioned, we see how little information is extracted and we recognise how high a price has been paid for this when we later find out Osborne has died.

CHECKPOINT 27

What error does the colonel make when speaking German?

The fact that Stanhope wishes to see the men after the raid and leaves the colonel to carry out the questioning of the prisoner shows that his loyalty is to his company. When he returns to the joyful colonel's news that 'It's a feather in our cap' (p. 79), his mood is sullen and a reluctant colonel is forced to ask about casualties. Stanhope's bitter words show his sadness and sense of loss at the deaths of Osborne and the six others: 'Still it'll be awfully nice if the brigadier's pleased' (p. 79). He clearly feels let down by his superiors and under his *'expressionless'* scrutiny the colonel *'fidgets uneasily'* (p. 79).

The tragedy of war

Raleigh's behaviour and appearance suggest the trauma he has endured. Even after the colonel congratulates him and promises him a Military Cross he is unable to speak. In response he merely *'sits with lowered head, looking at the palms of his hands'* (p. 80) which are covered in blood. Stanhope too is numb and silent; when he does speak his voice is *'expressionless and dead'* (p. 80). His pointed remark at Raleigh only adds to the tragedy of the scene as Raleigh is forced, in his shaken state, to stand with *'lowered head'* (p. 80) and heavy guns are heard in the background.

PART FOUR (PP. 80–8) – CELEBRATORY DINNER

1. The men sit eating and drinking; Raleigh is absent.

2. They discuss women.

3. The talk turns to Raleigh and the raid.

4. Hibbert is sent to bed.

5. Trotter is made second in command and Raleigh's meal is brought in.

Stanhope, Trotter and Hibbert open the scene with feverish laughter and conversation, a stark contrast to the tension of the preceding scene. Hibbert is seen in an unusually talkative mood, sharing his postcards of women with the others and making jokes. The mood is light as the men take comfort in food, alcohol and thoughts of home and women. The setting is like that of the Last Supper (in the Bible, the meal eaten by Jesus and his followers the night before his execution), with the men celebrating before they die. Stanhope's call for whisky on top of champagne is a reminder to us of the strain he is under.

When the conversation turns to Raleigh the mood of the scene changes as Stanhope learns of Raleigh's reason for being absent and hears the others praising him. His true emotional state is apparent when he says, 'Oh, for God's sake forget that ... raid! Think I want to talk about it?' (p. 85). Despite Hibbert's attempts to return the subject of conversation back to women, Stanhope's disregard and then anger kill the celebration as he turns on Hibbert, ordering him to bed. When Hibbert tries to confront him as he did earlier and privately, the tension breaks as Stanhope viciously repeats his command, 'Get out of here for God's sake!' (p. 86).

CHECKPOINT 28

What are your views of Hibbert now?

Stanhope, now left on stage with Trotter, confides in him as he used to Osborne, talking about Hibbert's 'repulsive little mind' (p. 87) and revealing his envy of Trotter's ability to stay calm. We are given a brief insight into Trotter's character when he says, 'Always the same am I? *(He sighs.)* Little you know' (p. 87), suggesting that he too hides his true feelings. Yet when he is told that he is now second in command, his commitment to his duty and loyalty to Stanhope are clear in his words 'I won't let you down' (p. 87).

> **CHECKPOINT 29**
>
> How does Trotter react to Hibbert's behaviour?

PART FIVE (PP. 88–91) – RALEIGH AND STANHOPE PART ON BAD TERMS

1. **Raleigh enters the dugout hesitantly.**
2. **Stanhope pulls him up over not eating with the other officers.**
3. **He is told to eat his dinner but says he cannot because of Osborne's death.**
4. **Stanhope becomes emotional and tells Raleigh to leave.**

When Raleigh enters the dugout it is clear that he is uncertain of the reception he will receive. The silence on stage and his halting speech suggest tension. Stanhope's disappointment in him is evident as he confronts him over his absence at dinner. Raleigh's attempts at explanation are shouted down as Stanhope loses control. The latter is clearly upset at Osborne's death. He is under so much strain that '*His hand trembles so violently that he can scarcely take the cigar between his teeth*' (p. 90) and we and Raleigh watch horrified.

> **CHECKPOINT 30**
>
> Why is Stanhope behaving so erratically?

After trying to apologise for seeking out Stanhope's company, Raleigh is bullied into a position where he bursts out emotionally, '*his voice … nearly breaking*' (p. 91). He explains his lack of appetite only to be faced with a maddened Stanhope who Sherriff describes in monstrous terms as having '*wide and staring*' (p. 91) eyes as he too fights for his breath under the emotions of the moment.

> **CHECKPOINT 31**
>
> What is the effect of Sherriff's use of personification at the end of the scene's directions?

The scene ends, as the directions indicate, with the personified sounds of war –'*the impatient grumble of gunfire that never dies away*' (p. 91), a reminder to us of the constant threat of attack that trench life brings.

Stanhope's revelation

Stanhope rarely reveals his true feelings; as a commander he must maintain morale and present himself as a leader. However in this scene, as with the Hibbert encounter, Stanhope shows his real feelings. In halting speech he reveals himself to Raleigh as a broken figure, suffering from the loss of his best friend and using drink to forget. Raleigh's apology does little to comfort Stanhope, who once again bursts out with an order of 'For God's sake, get out!' (p. 91).

PART SIX (PP. 92–6) – THE ATTACK BEGINS

1. **Mason wakes Stanhope.**
2. **Trotter enters in a cheery mood.**
3. **Stanhope sends a message to battalion headquarters and gives the sergeant major his orders.**
4. **The sound of shells grows closer.**
5. **Stanhope tells Trotter to take the others out to their platoons.**
6. **Trotter and Raleigh leave.**

It is five-thirty when Mason wakes Stanhope, who is only half asleep because of the cold. Trotter is already awake and has woken the others, showing that he is taking his role as second in command seriously.

CHECKPOINT 32

What is the significance of Trotter's singing?

His singing, and Stanhope's joke of giving him coins for it, lighten the mood as shells sound outside, suggesting the impending attack. Stanhope's joke over 'pâté de foie gras' (p. 95) is not understood by Mason, who clearly does not know what it is. These few moments of humour help to relieve the tension.

The sergeant major's report makes clear the danger of the situation. Stanhope's suggestion to him that all the men are given 'a decent drop of rum' (p. 94) as encouragement reminds us of Osborne and Raleigh before the raid. We expect a similar loss of lives, as we remember the fact that the company cannot expect any help from behind and must stick to their position. Stanhope's message to headquarters and request that there is no reply demonstrate his own expectations of tragedy.

With Stanhope's whisky at an end, we realise that the men's lives and the play are drawing to an end too. As Stanhope sits with *'quavering hand'* (p. 96) the events of the previous night seem forgotten as he and Raleigh exchange casual greetings before Raleigh leaves the dugout.

PART SEVEN (PP. 96–8) – HIBBERT DELAYS HIS DUTY

1. **Stanhope calls for Hibbert to join the others.**
2. **Hibbert sips his water slowly.**
3. **Mason and Hibbert leave together.**

By the time Hibbert is called, shells are falling steadily, indicating that the attack is in full swing. Hibbert's appearance suggests that he is terrified – *'He is very pale; he moves as if half asleep'* (p. 96) and later stage directions indicate that *'he is the picture of misery'* (p. 97).

DID YOU KNOW?

The average life expectancy of a junior officer in 1916 and 1917 was just six weeks.

GLOSSARY

pâté de foie gras delicacy made of goose liver

Hibbert's request for water and slow sips are evidently a ploy to delay his going out to the trench but Stanhope sees through him: 'You're just wasting as much time as you can' (p. 97). Cleverly, Stanhope tells Mason that Hibbert will guide him to the front line, forcing Hibbert to leave.

PART EIGHT (PP. 98–103) – RALEIGH DIES

① A soldier arrives with news from the front line.

② The sergeant major is told to take casualties to a dugout on the right.

③ News of Raleigh's injury arrives and Stanhope orders that he be brought to the dugout.

④ Raleigh is placed on Osborne's bed.

⑤ Stanhope talks to Raleigh as he dies.

When the soldier arrives with news from the front line it is clear that things are not going well. The discussion over where to put casualties shows that the facilities the soldiers had for dealing with the wounded were inadequate. Through all the discussions, shells are heard ominously sounding in the background. *'Flying fragments of shell whistle and hiss and moan overhead'* (p. 99) suggesting that the pace of the attack is increasing.

Just as Stanhope is preparing to join the others at the front, news of Raleigh's injury arrives; his command that he be brought to the dugout suggests the responsibility he feels towards Raleigh. As Raleigh is brought in Sherriff describes him being carried by the sergeant major *'like a child in his huge arms'* (p. 100). This **simile** highlights his youth and makes the tragedy of his impending death all the more acute. For Sherriff, he represents the hundreds and thousands of young soldiers who died in the First World War.

Significantly, Stanhope has made Osborne's bed ready for Raleigh and in his increasingly emotional state he contradicts his previous orders and asks that stretcher-bearers come and try to help Raleigh.

CHECKPOINT 33

What is the reason for Stanhope's placing of Raleigh on Osborne's bed?

Stanhope's tenderness towards Raleigh is clear as he looks after him and uses his first name – 'You've got a Blighty one, Jimmy' (p. 101). Raleigh's talk of rugby reminds us of his and Stanhope's shared history, and must offer some comfort to Raleigh. Meanwhile, Stanhope tries to make light of Raleigh's injury but the change in Raleigh's voice after he is unable to move his legs tells us that he has realised he is dying. The stage directions as Raleigh dies *'the faint rosy glow of dawn is deepening to an angry red'* (p. 102) reflect the worsening of events, just as Raleigh's last words are telling: 'it's so frightfully dark and cold' (p. 102). We may wonder whether in saying this, Raleigh is talking about the dugout or death itself.

The price of war

Stanhope's reaction is one of shock as he *'stares listlessly'* (p. 102) at Raleigh. This is the image of a man defeated by war and all it brings. The sounds of the attack, its anger and fury, make clear that the end is near, and as Stanhope leaves, having tenderly run his fingers over Raleigh's hair, the dugout is seen to collapse into darkness. Sherriff shows us the price of war. We are left believing that all the men have died, the *'red dawn'* (p. 103) symbolising their lost blood and the dull rattle of machine guns the continuing battle.

CHECKPOINT 34

How does Stanhope try to comfort Raleigh?

 CHECK THE BOOK

Read *Anthem for Doomed Youth* by Wilfred Owen. The opening lines of Owen's poem seem to echo the closing scene direction of the play.

CHECKPOINT 35

What is the mood of the closing scene?

GLOSSARY

Blighty one a wound which would get you sent home

TEST YOURSELF (ACT III)

Check your answers on p. 81.

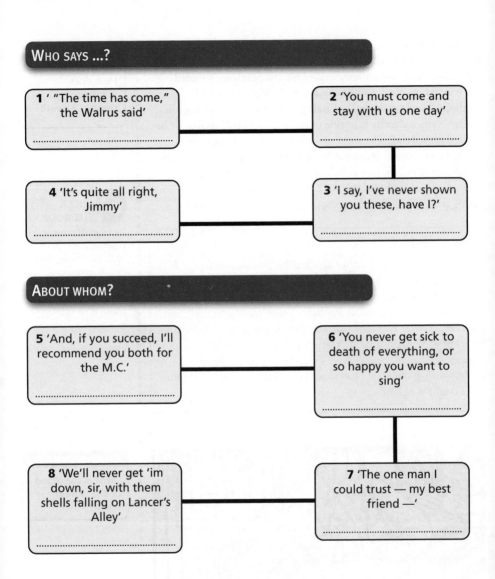

WHO SAYS ...?

1 ' "The time has come," the Walrus said'

....

2 'You must come and stay with us one day'

....

4 'It's quite all right, Jimmy'

....

3 'I say, I've never shown you these, have I?'

....

ABOUT WHOM?

5 'And, if you succeed, I'll recommend you both for the M.C.'

....

6 'You never get sick to death of everything, or so happy you want to sing'

....

8 'We'll never get 'im down, sir, with them shells falling on Lancer's Alley'

....

7 'The one man I could trust — my best friend —'

....

COMMENTARY

THEMES

WAR

When R. C. Sherriff wrote *Journey's End* he tried to show audiences 'how men really lived in the trenches' (*No Leading Lady*). He wanted people to recognise themselves, their friends, their sons and husbands in the characters on stage. He knew, as he wrote in his autobiography, that many of the men his audience would be thinking about 'had not returned'; the play was a tribute to them. The realism with which Sherriff conveys war is seen in the setting, the characters and events of the play.

The mud trenches, the rats, the endless waiting and the eerie quiet all contribute to this image of war which Sherriff knew would be familiar to many. He knew that audiences would recognise the stillness of the setting where there was 'not a sound or a soul ... yet you knew thousands of guns were hidden there ... thousands of Germans were waiting and thinking' (Act II, p. 43). They would also understand it when soldiers like Stanhope and Osborne are seen being forced to follow orders, unable to disobey their commanding officers or change events – 'Our orders are to stick here' (Act II, p. 50).

When the play was first staged the audience would have recognised Raleigh's youthful enthusiasm and Stanhope's hardened cynicism as typical reactions to the war. The apparent complacency of the colonel and his lack of interest in those killed after the raid would also have been familiar to those who had been at the front line. Raleigh arrives at the front with certain idealistic expectations about war and Osborne tries to preserve this image of war for him – 'Think of it all as — as romantic. It helps' (Act I, p. 16). Raleigh views his having been chosen to go on the raid as an honour: 'I say — it's most frightfully exciting!' (Act II, p. 65). Yet the raid changes him, as he begins to see what war really is.

The men are presented as worthy characters whose lives are sacrificed for no reasonably justifiable cause. The raid is only

EXAMINER'S SECRET
Try to include quotations in your sentences. It's better to use shorter and more precise quotations rather than long ones.

DID YOU KNOW?

37,000 M.C.s (Military Crosses) and 634 V.C.s (Victoria Crosses) were awarded during the First World War.

successful because a little information is extracted from the German prisoner and yet seven men die for this. When Osborne and Stanhope talk of worms and reflect over the fear they might feel in going the wrong way pointlessly, Sherriff uses the conversation as a metaphor for the men's feelings of hopelessness and futility. It is fitting that Osborne should escape into the world of *Alice in Wonderland*, where nothing seems to make sense, when he is in a world which seems to make no sense itself (see **Detailed summary** on Act II, p. 61).

For many the play came to be seen as anti-war. It was one of the only popular plays about war and as Swaffer, a critic of the time said, 'It carries a lesson – one that is nobly told' (*Daily Express*, 1928). Sherriff managed to expose the truth about war, despite not wishing to criticise it; he had himself been awarded a Military Cross for bravery.

Although Sherriff did not write *Journey's End* as an anti-war play, the fact that its characters are seen suffering emotionally, and are presented as physically wrecked and dying, is a reminder to audiences of the casualties of war. Many young, talented and educated men died in the First World War. They came to be known as the 'lost generation' and it is to them that *Journey's End* pays homage. David Grindley's recent West End production made clear this link when, at the end of the play, the entire company poignantly stood on stage before a marble cenotaph bearing names of the dead, signifying the wasteful horror of war.

CHECK THE BOOK

Robert Graves and Siegfried Sassoon both wrote autobiographies recording their experiences of war. Look out for *Goodbye to All That* and *Memoirs of an Infantry Soldier*.

HEROISM

Sherriff presents us with heroism in its various forms. Raleigh arrives at C Company having especially asked to join it because of his 'hero-worship' (p. 28) of Stanhope. He clearly views the war as an extension of school life where the 'skipper of Rugger' (p. 11) will lead him to victory on the battlefield. Indeed we are aware of Stanhope's heroism in wartime as he has a Military Cross himself. He has been at the front for the longest and is admired by his officers, in spite of his drinking. If this wasn't enough, his volunteering himself for the raid confirms him as a hero in the play.

However, despite Stanhope's own heroism, it is his knowledge of
the likelihood of death which makes him afraid for himself and
others. He wants to protect Raleigh from the truth and preserve
Raleigh's view of him as an unflawed hero. This causes Stanhope to
behave strangely towards him and try to censor his letter to Madge.
Osborne's view is that, despite Stanhope's fears, Raleigh's
admiration will continue – 'There's something deep and rather fine
about hero-worship' (p. 29). He is proved right when the contents
of Raleigh's letter are read out.

Sherriff presents us with two sides of the coin – the heroism and its
cost. It is only after his experience of the raid that Raleigh begins to
recognise the true price of glory. He has been exposed to the truth
and the futility of the attack, so that when he comes back to the
dugout he is described as *'walking as though he were asleep'* (p. 79).
He has been deadened by the experience. Yet it is because of his
actions in the raid that Raleigh becomes a hero. He is promised the
Military Cross – an award for bravery and heroism. However,
although the officers at dinner pay tribute to his courage, they
recognise its cost.

It is this recognition of the cost of war that earlier caused Stanhope's
fury at Hibbert. He views his cowardice as dishonourable, in the
light of others' bravery and heroism: 'If you went — and left
Osborne and Trotter and Raleigh and all those men up there to do
your work — could you ever look a man straight in the face again
— in all your life?' (p. 58). Part of the heroism of these men comes
from their unity in the face of difficulties. Stanhope's reliance on
volunteers for the raid shows the courage and heroism of his
company.

The deaths of Osborne and the others may be seen as pointless by
some, but in the face of difficulties and complacency – in the shape
of the colonel and his superiors – we must also view their deaths as
heroic. Sherriff recognises and pays tribute to the heroism of the
men of C Company. To him they represent all the men who died in
the First World War.

**DID YOU
KNOW?**

At the end of the
First World War,
908,371 British men
and women had
been killed and
2 million had been
injured; 1,773,700
Germans were killed
and 4 million
injured.

Like Stanhope, Sherriff views these men as worthy of loyalty and admiration – 'Don't you think it worth standing in with men like that?' (p. 58). For these men to work together as a team, only to give up their lives to certain death, requires courage and, as Sherriff ends the play, we are sadly reminded that the price paid for such heroism is blood: *'the red dawn glows through the jagged holes of the broken doorway'* (p. 103).

COMRADESHIP

Throughout the play we are presented with instances of comradeship and unity. The constant threat of death and the men's subsequent reliance on each other create this special bond. This is apparent throughout their time in the dugout.

When Raleigh first enters the play, Osborne takes him under his wing, explaining to him trench life. We are told that Osborne is known as 'uncle' (p. 10) suggesting his older age and the close family-like relationship the soldiers share. Trotter is equally welcoming to Raleigh and we see their fondness for each other in their comments to other officers.

It is apparent that Osborne is close to many of the officers: he and Trotter share memories of gardening; he and Raleigh talk of home and rugby. Their closeness is reinforced when they are both selected for the raid. Osborne is also the one in whom Mason confides over the tinned pineapple error. Osborne is the one to whom Stanhope talks frankly about the war, about Raleigh and about life. He and Stanhope are evidently good friends. Osborne tells Hardy, 'I love that fellow. I'd go to hell with him' (p. 7). Osborne is second in command and, as Stanhope later admits, his 'best friend' (p. 91). Stanhope's clear distress at Osborne's loss demonstrates the friendship between the two of them. In fact, his loss is a severe blow to the whole company.

Raleigh and Stanhope knew each other at school and are family friends. This makes Stanhope's position difficult and causes a great deal of conflict in the play. However their true bond is evident at the end of the play when Raleigh is injured. Significantly Stanhope

DID YOU KNOW?

Trenches were about seven feet deep and six feet wide.

DID YOU KNOW?

Rum was the alcohol given to soldiers. Each division of 20,000 men had 300 gallons of rum which was distributed in cold weather and after an attack.

prepares Osborne's (his best friend's) bed for Raleigh, a bed he had earlier told Raleigh to get off, and he stays with him till his death.

It is this special bond and friendship between men that Stanhope draws on when trying to persuade Hibbert to stay – 'Shall we see if we can stick it together?' (p. 57) – and it is this comradeship which leads us to believe that not one but all of them will die at the end of the play.

PUBLIC SCHOOL AND CLASS

All the officers, except for Trotter, have attended public schools and speak in an upper class accent. Trotter obviously stands out because of this and even Raleigh comments on how he makes things seem 'natural' (p. 39). At the start of the First World War, only men who had been to public schools could become commissioned officers. However, the class system was changing and by the end of the first year of war the traditional officer class no longer existed. It was possible to gain promotion without having been educated privately. Sherriff himself became a captain in the East Surrey Regiment in this way.

In *Journey's End*, the central focus on public school life, with talk of rugby, cricket and schoolmasters, acts as a bond between the men. It allows them to view life at the front as an extension of school life. At the time, public schools were single-sex boarding establishments, so for men to live and work together in the small space of a dugout would not have been that different from their schooldays, where they would have shared rooms with others. The importance of this shared background is clear: Osborne measures distances by relating them to rugby fields and Raleigh relates his fatal injury to one he suffered in rugby. Osborne can be seen to be like an old and wise housemaster, Stanhope a head boy and Raleigh a newcomer who needs to learn the rules of school life: 'I know you're new to this but I thought you'd have the common sense to leave the men alone to their meals' (p. 89). Stanhope evidently sees a clear divide between the officers and the other men – 'My officers are here to be respected – not laughed at' (p. 89). Raleigh's eating with the ordinary soldiers is not acceptable and for this he must be told off, in the same way that Hibbert's failure to perform his duty requires

DID YOU KNOW?

When David Grindley directed his West End production of *Journey's End* in 2004, he took care not to portray Trotter as a stereotypical man of his class.

DID YOU KNOW?

Sherriff was turned down by the first college he applied to at Oxford University because he had not learned Latin. With the help of a friend, he was admitted to Oxford as a special student, only to leave the following year.

punishment. For Trotter to be promoted to second in command after Osborne's death is evidence of the way the class system was beginning to change. In this new system it was possible for individuals to succeed by merit and not because of birth.

STRUCTURE

EXAMINER'S SECRET

When writing about a specific scene or extract try to link it to the rest of the play. This way, you will demonstrate knowledge of the whole play.

The play has three acts with everything taking place over four days. The confined timespan, the claustrophobic setting and the overwhelming feeling of doom help to create a sense of unity in the play.

Because of the play's realism, some critics have accused it of having no structure: 'The play is a series of scenes almost unrelated and as difficult of interpretation as they would be in real life' (*The Times*, 1929). The apparently disorganised nature of events is surely a reflection of the chaos of war where things do not follow a strict pattern. Even when George Bernard Shaw first read the play he maintained that it was 'properly speaking a document, not a drama'.

Vivian Summers in her analysis of the play said that it was not a 'well made play' (*Penguin Passnotes*) and strictly speaking the play does not follow the traditional format of a well made play. Events do not fit neatly together nor do they lead naturally on to the next. The audience is left not knowing what to think. Rather, what Sherriff does is include a number of complications, moments of drama and an exploration of characters' reactions and relationships, showing the conditions of war. He leaves the audience to come to its own conclusions.

DID YOU KNOW?

Sherriff's autobiography, *No Leading Lady*, is called this because *Journey's End* is an all-male play with no leading lady.

Sherriff introduces characters and setting in the first act, and suggests a potential complication with the inclusion of Raleigh. However, some critics feel that this part of the plot is not realistic. Sherriff then builds up towards a mini-climax with the conflict over the letter. This is resolved by halfway through Act II when the next complication is introduced – the raid and the potential threat to the lives of those closest to Stanhope. The next dramatic moment occurs when there is a conflict between Hibbert and Stanhope (no doubt anxious about the raid). By the end of this act the audience is left expectant. In the first scene of the third and final act the raid has already taken place and Osborne has died. Following this, another quarrel occurs, this time between Stanhope and Raleigh. Finally, in the last scene of the play, Raleigh, and we may assume the others, die.

If we approach the structure of the play in terms of mood, we can see that Sherriff varies this to great effect. He moves from moments of calm to tension, light relief to drama, joy to sadness, and anger to peace. He may not have been following the traditional format of a well made play but he showed an acute awareness of theatre as stage performance. He recognised that, given all the action of the play was limited to the one setting of the dugout, the events of war would have to be indicated through sounds and lighting. He wrote in *No Leading Lady*, 'everything depended upon the realism of the sounds of war outside'. He also recognised a range of emotions would be necessary both to maintain the interest of spectators and to present a realistic view of war. This was partly due to the limitations and size of the setting in the dugout, and because of the resultant claustrophobia. The war setting allowed him to include extremes of emotion. In stressful situations, strained emotions are to be expected. In creating a play which leapt from high drama to calm, Sherriff showed a true understanding of human psychology and of the war itself.

Sherriff includes Mason and food as light relief; Osborne as friend to all; and a range of character types that cut across classes and events, thus taking audiences on an emotional journey. In this way Sherriff was able to create what was, after all, both a commercially successful play and one that has stood the test of time. Since its first performance in 1928, it has been revived on countless occasions, most recently in 2004.

EXAMINER'S SECRET
Plot a graph following the mood of events in the play. This will help you to see how the emotions of the play change. Consider whether these are linked to the emotions of any particular character.

Characters

Stanhope

Captain Stanhope is the son of a vicar and commander of C Company. He is first introduced through Hardy and Osborne's conversation at the start of the play. The first impression we gain of him is of a heavy drinker – 'a freak show' (p. 5) – but clearly someone who commands loyalty. This is obvious from Osborne's defence of him – 'He's a long way the best company commander we've got' (p. 4). The fact that he has not taken proper leave in three years indicates his attitude to duty and his strength of character. He believes that the well-being and morale of the whole company is more important than one man.

It is clear that his experiences at war have affected him. When he first appears the stage directions state that *'Although tanned by months in the open air, there is a pallor under his skin and dark shadows under his eyes'* (p. 17). He later admits to Osborne that the reason he has not returned home since the battle at Vimy Ridge is because he does not wish Madge to see him as he has become. He wants to 'get fit' (p. 29) before he goes back to her again. He is clearly upset at seeing Raleigh and recognises the threat that his presence poses. This shows how much he cares for Madge. He wishes to protect her from the truth. By introducing a love interest, Sherriff allows the audience to feel some tenderness for a man who could otherwise have been seen as harsh and uncaring.

It is evident that his company and others (Hardy included) recognise Stanhope's standards. His 'carefully brushed hair' and 'well cared for' (p. 17) uniform show this. He clearly thinks that hygiene and tidiness are important; this is understandable given the circumstances, where lack of organisation could cost lives. Hardy is obviously aware of this, hence his speedy exit. As predicted, when Stanhope enters the dugout he complains about the 'blasted mess those fellows left the trenches in' (p. 17). This is closely followed by a request for whisky. His reaction to Raleigh shows us that Stanhope views his presence as an unnecessary complication in an already strained situation. He feels a responsibility towards Raleigh

Strict
Dutiful
Strained
Experienced
Hardened

EXAMINER'S SECRET
A good way to study characters is to list about four adjectives to describe each and find some quotations from the play to support these adjectives.

and recognises the need to protect him, yet feels he cannot do so under the circumstances. He is clearly not happy with having been surprised and resents Raleigh's presence, despite the fact that Raleigh has evidently gone to great lengths to join his company. This in itself shows us that Stanhope is a man worthy of admiration; Raleigh 'hero worships' (p. 28) Stanhope and has deliberately sought out C Company. It is clear both to the audience and Stanhope that Raleigh recognises his commander's true worth. This is shown from Raleigh's comments both to Osborne, and surprisingly in the letter to his sister.

What Stanhope demonstrates is true leadership qualities, those that the public schools of the time sought to cultivate in young men. It is obvious from their accents that all the officers in his company, except Trotter, went to public schools. In fact, the original inspiration for Sherriff's play came from the beginnings of a novel that he had written in which the lives of two main characters were followed from their public school through to working life. In his autobiography, Sherriff wrote of Stanhope, 'Dennis had everything a boy desired: good looks and charm, supreme ability for games and a gift for leadership' (*No Leading Lady*).

EXAMINER'S SECRET
Remember that what someone says, thinks and does are all indicators of character. What others say and think about them will also suggest their character.

At the age of only twenty-one, Stanhope is leading a company of men, some older than he is and he has won a Military Cross (p. 28). It is clear that his experiences at the battle for Vimy Ridge, where there had been heavy losses, have driven him to drink – to break 'the strain' (p. 28). However, the fact that he can rely on volunteers for the raiding party shows the loyalty he is still able to command.

Similarly, when faced with Hibbert's attempt to leave, Stanhope is able to persuade him to stay. Only someone who was truly respected would be able to handle events in this way. It is true, however, that we may see Stanhope's initial threat of shooting Hibbert as unreasonable. There are instances throughout the play where Stanhope's strained nerves are evident, making us less sympathetic to him. For example, Mason clearly fears some sort of punishment over the pineapple chunks error, and Stanhope forces Raleigh to hand over his letter. He accuses Raleigh of being a fool for eating with the men and not the officers. However his ability to lead is unquestionable. He always places duty and the good of the entire company above all else.

Like any captain in wartime, he has to issue and follow orders, so to question the colonel's suggestion of Raleigh for the raid and to apologise to Osborne when telling him about it shows us that Stanhope has human qualities too. These human qualities are seen from time to time throughout the play. When Stanhope says to Raleigh 'You think there's no limit to what a man can bear?' (p. 91) we recognise that he is human after all. Sherriff presents Stanhope not as a perfect being but as a man with weaknesses and this endears him to the audience, restoring him as a hero. His bitter reaction at Osborne's death and his tenderness towards Raleigh as he dies make us feel that, even at the end of the play, Raleigh would most probably have said 'I'm awfully proud to think he's my friend' (p. 48).

RALEIGH

Raleigh is the youngest of the officers in C Company. He is a *'healthy looking'* (p. 9) and handsome second lieutenant to Stanhope, who was his hero when he was at school with him. Presented as naïve and inexperienced, straight out of school, he is an idealist who views war as 'romantic' (p. 16).

Young
Inexperienced
Naïve
Eager
Adaptable

When he first appears, he is described as having a *'boyish voice'* (p. 9) and hesitant speech, which indicate his lack of experience. Raleigh's youthful enthusiasm is evident through his exclamations and expressions of awe – 'She'll be awfully glad I'm with him here' (p. 13). His eager anticipation of meeting his hero Stanhope and his expectations about the war show that he views it as a continuation of boarding school. Sherriff deliberately includes references to rugby. Raleigh's enthusiasm at discovering that Osborne played for England – 'They ought to know. It'd make them feel jolly bucked' (p. 38) as well as his earlier joy at the prospect of playing soccer (p. 11) show his innocence. These also underline his unrealistic expectations of life at the front.

Despite Osborne's warnings about Stanhope, Raleigh is still shocked when he first meets him and on seeing him drunk later that night. Stanhope's behaviour over the letter further surprises Raleigh. His embarrassment about the contents shows his character. His persistent admiration for Stanhope is evident in his letter and this is made to seem all the greater because of Stanhope's misgivings.

His pride at having been chosen to go on the raid is contrasted with Osborne's resigned acceptance of his fate. We are therefore shown the difference between wisdom and inexperience. It is only once Raleigh comes back from the raid, having seen Osborne and six others killed, that his views change. His romantic ideals are shattered as he comes to recognise the truth about war. He may have won a medal for bravery but he has lost a comrade and seen six others die and for what? A small amount of information extracted from a German prisoner. The other officers come to view Raleigh with admiration, Hibbert even saying that he is 'too keen on his "duty"' (p. 85), but his inability to celebrate with the officers and his outburst at Stanhope show how upset he is. He feels guilty and confused by everything. Yet, like the others, he is not afraid to face the coming danger. The following day when the attack begins he joins Trotter and the others at the front, fully aware of the likelihood that they will be killed. He is still prepared to do his duty: even on his deathbed he says to Stanhope, 'I feel rotten lying here — everybody else — up there' (p. 101).

It seems that what Osborne says at the start of the play is proven true, 'I hope we're lucky and get a youngster straight from school. They're the kind that do best' (p. 3).

OSBORNE

Osborne is the oldest member of C Company. He is around forty-five years old, married and has two children. A former schoolmaster, he is second in command. Physically he is described *'as hard as nails'* (p. 1) and yet his character is calm and controlled, 'quiet and sober' (p. 4) as Hardy says.

He is a dutiful officer and very loyal to Stanhope, whom he recognises has suffered under the strain of leadership and three years' service at the front. The two of them are close; Stanhope

EXAMINER'S SECRET
Don't just write what a character does or says; explain what this shows.

Married
Middle-aged
Wise
Approachable
Loyal

confides in him and thinks of him as his best friend. Whilst Osborne recognises his commander's flaws, he still respects him.

Osborne's role as an adviser is made clear to us when we are told of his title of 'uncle' (p. 10) among the officers. We may see this partly as an extension of his role as a schoolmaster and because of his age. We also see this in practice in his conversations with Raleigh at the start of the play and later with Stanhope and Trotter.

He is evidently a humble individual who, despite having played rugby for England, does not boast about his achievements. He prefers to get on with his duties in a quiet way. His reading of *Alice in Wonderland* and enjoyment of gardening suggest that he is intelligent and thoughtful. When he is told that he is to go on the raid, he accepts his fate although he knows the potential dangers. He is protective of Raleigh and does not let him know his real thoughts about the raid. The reason he gives for taking off his wedding ring is that he does not want to lose it, rather than that he expects to be killed.

He is obviously a well-liked and trusted officer and his loss marks a turning point in the play. Raleigh's visions of war are altered: he is confused and moved, and Stanhope has lost his best friend.

TROTTER

Trotter is the only officer who has obviously not been to public school. He is middle-aged and *'homely looking'*. He is described as having a *'red, fat and round'* face and his tunic is *'on the verge of bursting at the waist'* (p. 17). He has clearly put on weight during the war. He eats for comfort, in the way that Stanhope drinks. He is evidently not in good physical shape and for this reason he is not chosen for the raid. However, he is a friendly character who is welcoming to Raleigh when he first arrives and who talks jovially amongst the officers, joking and relieving tension at times.

Friendly
Dutiful
Fat
Humorous

His love of gardening, his age and marriage provide a bond between him and Osborne who share memories of home. He is presented as an unemotional individual who uses humour and food to relieve stress. Yet we are given an indication when he talks to Stanhope after Osborne's death that there is more to him than first appears.

Trotter does not share as strong a bond with Stanhope as Osborne does, for his and Stanhope's relationship is more formal. However, when he is made second in command his commitment and loyalty are seen. He evidently feels honoured by the promotion and promises Stanhope that he will do his best and not let him down.

HIBBERT

When Hibbert is first introduced he is described as *'small'* and *'slightly built'* (p. 24). He is in his early twenties and has a moustache and pale face. Everything about him suggests a weak and ineffectual individual. From the very start he complains about a lack of appetite and goes to bed rather than join in the meal and the conversation. Sherriff immediately establishes him as someone who is not contributing fully to the team, and because of this, we do not feel sympathy for him.

Stanhope views him unsympathetically as a 'worm' and 'an artful little swine' (p. 25), trying to get home; he immediately assumes he is faking his illness. We may be inclined to agree with him but Osborne's more controlled opinion provides a balancing view.

Weak
Scared
Crude
Desperate

We gain little direct insight into Hibbert until he argues with Stanhope, when it becomes clear that Hibbert is suffering psychologically. The fact that Stanhope has to threaten and then manipulate him into staying shows the extent both of his mental anguish, and his lack of care for the other officers. On the one hand we are moved by Hibbert's suffering but on the other we realise that he is failing to do his duty in difficult circumstances.

The other characters view Hibbert negatively: Stanhope obviously dislikes him and Trotter calls him a 'funny little bloke' (p. 65). Only Osborne who is aware of his weaknesses, and Raleigh, who is a newcomer, do not judge him.

Sherriff presents Hibbert unfavourably throughout the play, but this is particularly clear at the meal after Osborne's death. Hibbert demonstrates his true character by showing the other men rude pictures and boasting about his exploits with women. Trotter's remarks to him show that he is behaving strangely and it is clear that he is drunk. This has made him unusually talkative. When he refers to Raleigh as being 'too keen on his duty' (p. 85), we are reminded of his own inadequacies in this area. At the end of the play any sympathy he had gained earlier by agreeing to stay is soon lost when he fails to perform his duty by deliberately wasting time. This provides a fitting contrast to Raleigh who, despite his argument with Stanhope the previous night, willingly joins his platoon at the front, eventually sacrificing his life.

COLONEL

Complacent
Insensitive
Ambitious
Tactical

The colonel does not appear on stage for very long, yet he is important to the action of the play. He serves as a symbol of those complacent decision-makers who show little regard for human life. He views war as a game where all that matters is obeying orders and gaining 'a feather' in one's 'cap' (p. 79).

Despite this, he agrees with Stanhope regarding the timing of the raid, but he is unable to convince the general of this. He is less close to C Company and obviously does not feel as strongly as Stanhope. He concludes rather dismissively that 'I've done all I can' (p. 67) and insists, as his general does, that 'present arrangements have got to stand' (p. 66).

Tactically, his selection of officers for the raid makes sense, and we cannot blame him for having to follow orders. We lose sympathy for him because of his gleeful and insensitive response to the very small amount of information he obtains from the German prisoner. He fails to enquire about casualties after the raid, and is obviously uncomfortable when talking to Stanhope. Putting it simply, he is the bad guy who we feel comfortable blaming for the loss of our familiar and well-liked Osborne.

EXAMINER'S SECRET
Being able to see two sides of a character or interpret something in two ways will get you higher marks.

MASON

Mason is of a lower class to the officers. He acts as their cook and servant, but is also a fighting soldier. This is seen at the end of the play when he joins the others at the front, accompanied by a reluctant Hibbert.

We do not get a great deal of information about his appearance but we gain an impression of his character from his actions. He is evidently hard-working and keen to serve: he never questions his orders. His concern over having got the wrong tin of fruit and his reaction to the mix-up over pepper show his loyalty to his company. Osborne and Trotter discussing his dirty dishcloth provides some light relief in the play but also gives us an indication of the inadequate facilities at the front. Mason serves as a reminder that normal activities still have to continue despite the war. As well as food, he also provides a much-needed break from the tension of the war.

HARDY

Hardy is only seen at the beginning of the play. He provides our first insight into Stanhope. Hardy himself is clearly messy and disorganised, providing a contrast with Stanhope when he appears later. He also allows an early insight into Osborne as a character and lays the foundations for our expectations both of characters and setting.

LANGUAGE AND STYLE

REALISM

In the late nineteenth century a new form of drama emerged, one that showed people in their natural environments. Realism, as it came to be known, depicted real life and everyday situations with actors behaving naturally and not acting in a stylised way. *Journey's End* is this type of play. In his autobiography, R. C. Sherriff wrote that 'a play came easily because you simply had to use the words that people spoke in everyday life' (*No Leading Lady*).

Whilst some may regard the language of the text now as dated, it is realistic. Words like 'cheero' (p. 8), 'old chap' (p. 60), 'rugger' and 'skipper' (p. 11) place the play firmly in its setting and era. It is the language of the 1920s public schoolboy, the language of the typical army officer of the time.

Working class
Dutiful

Red-faced
Cheerful
Messy
Disorganised

Only Mason and Trotter do not use this language and this sets them apart in terms of class (see the sections on **Character** and **Public school and class**).

- MASON AND TROTTER. Mason speaks in a Cockney (London) accent and Sherriff indicates this in the spelling and dropped letters at the beginnings and ends of words. The meat Mason serves at the start of the play has a 'noo shape' and 'smells like liver … but it 'asn't got that smooth wet look' (p. 9). Trotter also speaks differently from the other officers. He uses phrases such as 'I reckon' (p. 36) where Raleigh and the others say 'I suppose' (p. 42). His exclamations are more frequent and consist of words such as 'bloomin'' (p. 33), 'blinkin'' (p. 36) and 'damn' (p. 36) where the other officers say things like 'beastly'(p. 57), 'frightfully' (p. 37) and, on occasion, 'damned' (p. 27).

  He is seen by the others as a 'genuine sort of chap' who 'makes things feel natural' (p. 39) and this may be due to his less formal speech. Stanhope thinks he has no imagination and believes that he cannot see beyond a 'surface' (p. 42). Perhaps he thinks this because of Trotter's straightforward speech.

  Trotter uses colloquialisms and idioms, often in a crude way. When he hears of the raid which Osborne and Raleigh are to lead, he recounts the story of the red rags and the previous raid. He talks of it as being 'murder' (p. 62), by which he means that it was difficult. However, with the likelihood of people being killed, his words have a double meaning. As a result of this raid, some men would have literally been murdered. In which case, his words are ill-chosen, as they are too near to the truth for comfort. For this reason, Osborne advises him not to tell Raleigh 'it's murder' (p. 63).

  Similarly, Trotter's simple and crude rhymes contrast with Osborne's meaningful references to *Alice in Wonderland*. Trotter recites, 'Tell me, mother, what is that / That looks like strawberry jam?'/ 'Hush, hush my dear; 'tis only Pa / Run over by a tram …' (p. 62) with its obvious reference to death. Osborne, on the other hand, talks of the 'gently smiling jaws' of 'the little crocodile' (p. 64), with a more subtle reference to life and death The two officers have very different ways of expressing their

reactions to the war. One explicitly refers to the situation; the other refers to it in a more controlled and implicit way, typical of most of the characters in the play.

- OSBORNE. Osborne is a calm character, something which is evident in his controlled language and reserved words. He shows little emotion in the play. The only explicit signs of emotion are in his defence of Stanhope at the start of the play and in his reaction to Stanhope's actions towards Raleigh, 'Good Heavens, Stanhope!' (p. 46). Like most of the officers in the play he deals with his emotions in a controlled manner.

- STANHOPE. As a captain, Stanhope must act in a restrained way. Most of his statements in front of the officers consist of orders and gaining or giving information. It is only when he is speaking to Osborne and at moments of tension that we see how Stanhope's nerves are 'battered' (p. 6). His state of mind reveals itself in a number of outbursts. His bitterness is apparent in his references to a 'worm' (p. 25), 'prigs' (p. 90) and 'shirkers' (p. 55). All these words show the contempt with which he views people who do not contribute to the team. However, these words are used when Stanhope speaks in confidence to others or when he is feeling extreme emotion. They reveal the hardened cynicism of a man who has been at the front for three years and can no longer contain his emotions.

- RALEIGH. Raleigh's words reveal his innocence. His initial nervousness and hesitant speech, his use of words like 'Rather!' (p. 35), 'I say, really!' (p. 38) and 'How topping!' (p. 38) show him to be an impressionable character. His enthusiastic approach to life at the front makes clear that he views it as an exciting adventure.

Understatement, irony and humour

R. C. Sherriff makes his characters deliberately use very controlled language. This not only reflects the image of the British with their 'stiff upper lip' but suggests the way that the men come to treat an abnormal situation in a normal way. War comes to be part of everyday life for them. The characters' use of understatement shows how normal the war has become. For example, Hardy says

EXAMINER'S SECRET
Keep focused on the question you have been set, and make sure that everything you write is relevant to it. Answer the question!

that the men were 'frightfully annoyed' (p. 2) that their dugout had been blown to bits and Raleigh refers to the destruction of trenches and lives as 'silly' (p. 39).

This use of understatement serves also as a device to hide painful emotion, in the same way that humour and irony are used in the play. Osborne replies to Hardy's understatement at the start of the play by saying, 'There's nothing worse than dirt in your tea' (p. 2). Clearly the fact that the dugout has been blown up is of greater significance than dirt in one's tea, but Osborne uses the humour to enable him to deal with the horror of war. In the same way Stanhope's bitterly ironic remark after Osborne's death helps him to cope with his loss: 'How awfully nice — if the brigadier's pleased' (p. 79). Trotter's rather more crude humour with his attempt at word play when he refers to the cutlet not letting him 'cut it' (p. 24) is more in keeping with his less apparently sophisticated character.

DID YOU KNOW?

By the end of the First World War, the British army had dealt with 80,000 cases of shell shock.

Sherriff's controlled language and use of pauses and silences allow us to sense what is left unsaid. Tension is deepened because of the silences and pauses and the characters' use of simple language can conceal deep feelings. This is very apparent when Osborne is told of the raid by Stanhope. Osborne's short, clipped sentences suggest his shock and anxiety. He repeatedly says, 'I see' (p. 60) and 'Yes' in reply to the other's statements. The implication is that he is leaving a lot unsaid.

INFERENCE, SYMBOLISM AND IMAGERY

DID YOU KNOW?

During the First World War, as well as the British and German soldiers who died, over 5 million soldiers from Europe, Turkey, Australia and America died.

Where Sherriff succeeds most effectively is in his use of inference and symbolism. We can infer from Osborne's 'I see' (p. 60) when he is told of the raid that he is resigned to his fate. In the same way, we may infer, when he and Stanhope talk of worms earlier that they are a metaphor for their feelings of hopelessness. The crocodile in Osborne's recitation from *Alice in Wonderland* serves as a symbol of war, one which deceives and kills. When Trotter hears the rhyme he says, 'I don't see no point in that' and Osborne replies, 'Exactly. That's just the point' (p. 64). The artfulness of the crocodile, and hence war, is its ability to deceive. Similarly, the apparent pointlessness of the rhyme is its very truth. What Osborne is saying is that as far as he can see there is no point to war. The world in which he and the others find themselves is a nonsense world like that in *Alice in Wonderland*; the text becomes a metaphor for their own lives.

Other images appear through the words of the characters, particularly when describing the front. Trotter talks of the quiet by likening it to 'an empty 'ouse' (p. 20) and Stanhope says that 'you could have heard a pin drop' (p. 43) in it. Both images create an impression for the audience of the deathly stillness of the setting. Sherriff heightens the irony of this unnatural world by making his characters compare life at the front to life away from the front and to natural objects, 'gas that smells like pear drops' (p. 36). Stanhope's powerful simile describing the state of the trenches as being 'all churned up like a sea that's got muddier and muddier till it's so stiff that it can't move' (p. 43) creates a vivid image of a chaotic world swallowing all in its path. It has reached a point where there seems to be no way out. This image is later developed by Sherriff in the end scene when the falling shells are likened to '*an angry sea*' (p. 103).

Sherriff's use of light and staging is skilfully symbolic. The stage and its directions come to reflect the characters' feelings. We see Stanhope move to shadows on stage when he wants to conceal himself because of sadness or shame. The significance of red lights being used to suggest danger or death is also apparent. The sound of war is personified, described in terms of a 'whine' and 'great fury' (p. 103). This again suggests the connection between man and war. It may also imply that, once started, war takes on a life of its own. It becomes an unnatural life-form whose hunger can only be satisfied by death.

Sherriff's skill as a playwright allowed *Journey's End* to succeed where other plays had failed. As Baz Kershaw said 'no play of the period so successfully depicted the degradation of war as R. C. Sherriff's *Journey's End*' (*Cambridge History of British Theatre, Volume 3 – Since 1985*).

EXAMINER'S SECRET

In an exam, demonstrate that you know the social and historical background of the play and draw some parallels between the play and other books or poems. Showing examiners that you have read widely will impress them!

CHECK THE BOOK

As a contrast to the anti-war poetry you may have read, look at some poems by Jessie Pope, a pro-war female poet who wrote from the comfort of Britain, having never experienced war at the front. Look at *Who's for the Game?* especially.

CHECK THE BOOK

Read *The Soldier* by Rupert Brooke. The sentiments of the poem echo Raleigh's initial attitude to the war. Brooke died in 1915 and did not live to see the full horror of the First World War.

RESOURCES

HOW TO USE QUOTATIONS

EXAMINER'S SECRET

In a typical exam essay, you could use as many as eight quotations.

One of the secrets of success in writing essays is to use quotations effectively. There are five basic principles:

❶ Put inverted commas at the beginning and end of the quotation.

❷ Write the quotation exactly as it appears in the original.

❸ Do not use a quotation that repeats what you have just written.

❹ Use the quotation so that it fits into your sentence.

❺ Keep the quotation as short as possible.

Quotations should be used to develop the line of thought in your essays. Your comment should not duplicate what is in your quotation. For example:

Hardy tells Osborne that it must be difficult for him being second in command, given his sensible and older character, 'Poor old man. It must be pretty rotten for you, being his second in command, and you such a quiet, sober old thing' (Act I, p. 4).

It is far more effective to write:

Hardy suggests that it must be difficult for Osborne to be second to Stanhope because he is a 'quiet, sober old thing' (Act I, p. 4).

However the most sophisticated way of using the writer's words is to embed them into your sentence:

Hardy remarks that, given Osborne is a 'quiet, sober old thing', **it must be** 'pretty rotten' **for him to be** 'second in command' **to Stanhope** (Act I, p. 4).

When you use quotations in this way, you are demonstrating the ability to use text as evidence to support your ideas – not simply including words from the original to prove you have read it.

COURSEWORK ESSAY

Set aside an hour or so at the start of your work to plan what you have to do.

- List all the points you feel are needed to cover the task. Collect page references of information and quotations that will support what you have to say. A helpful tool is the highlighter pen: this saves painstaking copying and enables you to target precisely what you want to use.

- Focus on what you consider to be the main points of the essay. Try to sum up your argument in a single sentence, which could be the closing sentence of your essay. Depending on your essay title, it could be a statement about a character: Hibbert is presented unfavourably throughout the play. His cowardice is contrasted with the nobility and heroism of the others who serve their country regardless of their personal fears and ultimately sacrifice their lives; an opinion about setting: I believe that the claustrophobic nature of the trenches and the war situation helps to create an intimacy between the soldiers and a special bond of camaraderie; or a judgement on a theme: I think the main theme in *Journey's End* is the wasteful horror of war. Throughout the play we see the emotional and physical impact of war on individuals and, at the end of it, having grown familiar with characters, we are left believing that all of them have died.

- Make a short essay plan. Use the first paragraph to introduce the argument you wish to make. In the following paragraphs develop this argument with details, examples and other possible points of view. Sum up your argument in the last paragraph. Check you have answered the question.

- Write the essay, remembering all the time the central point you are making.

- On completion, make sure you go back over what you have written to eliminate careless errors and improve expression. Read it aloud to yourself, or, if you are feeling more confident, to a relative or friend.

EXAMINER'S SECRET
If you are asked to compare, remember to use words that suggest comparison and contrast such as, 'similarly', 'on the other hand', 'whereas', 'likewise' and 'however'.

EXAMINER'S SECRET
To do well you do not have to write a long essay. A good, analytical essay of two sides could get you an excellent mark.

If you can, try to type your essay, using a word processor. This will allow you to correct and improve your writing without spoiling its appearance.

SITTING THE EXAMINATION

Examination papers are carefully designed to give you the opportunity to do your best. Follow these handy hints for exam success:

BEFORE YOU START

EXAMINER'S SECRET

Always read through the whole paper before you start writing.

- Make sure that you know the subject of the examination so that you are properly prepared and equipped.

- You need to be comfortable and free from distractions. Inform the invigilator if anything is off-putting, e.g. a shaky desk.

- Read the instructions, or rubric, on the front of the examination paper. You should know by now what you need to do but check to reassure yourself.

- Observe the time allocation – and follow it carefully. If they recommend 60 minutes for Question 1 and 30 minutes for Question 2, it is because Question 1 carries twice as many marks.

- Consider the mark allocation. You should write a longer response for 4 marks than for 2 marks.

WRITING YOUR RESPONSES

EXAMINER'S SECRET

Keep an eye on the clock and don't run over time for any section of the paper.

- Use the questions to structure your response, e.g. question: 'The opening act of the play is dramatically effective. Explain its importance with reference to setting, characters and themes.' The first part of your answer will describe the opening act of the play; the second part will be an explanation of its significance. You should write a paragraph each on setting, characters and themes.

- Write a brief outline of your response.

- A typical thirty minutes examination essay is probably between 400 and 600 words in length.

- Keep your writing legible and easy to read, using paragraphs to show the structure of your answers.

- Spend a couple of minutes afterwards quickly checking for obvious errors.

WHEN YOU HAVE FINISHED

- Don't be downhearted – if you found the examination difficult, it is probably because you really worked at the questions. Let's face it, they are not meant to be easy!

- Don't pay too much attention to what your friends have to say about the paper. Everyone's experience is different and no two people ever give the same answers.

IMPROVE YOUR GRADE

A good essay will show that you understand various aspects of the play. You will need to show that you have a good knowledge of events, when things happen and how they are organised.

You should be able to show that you know what characters are like, how they are revealed to us, what they say and do and what others say about them. You should also be able to show that you understand relationships between characters and how they change during the course of the play.

You should be aware of how the playwright creates a particular atmosphere through stage lighting, furnishings and the way characters react to each other, as well as any other special effects.

You should have some knowledge of how the writer has been influenced by his/ her own life events and character/ aspirations. The views and opinions the writer expresses may reflect or contradict other people's views. You need to consider the writer's views and comment on the social and historical context in which the writer was working.

EXAMINER'S SECRET
Make sure you plan your points and always check your answer.

EXAMINER'S SECRET

Always refer to the text as a play and show an understanding of how a real audience would react to events, characters and themes.

IMPROVING YOUR RESPONSE FROM A D TO A C

In order to gain a D grade, you would need to:

- Begin to develop a response which focuses on the question
- Begin to show understanding of the play and its context
- Support your comments with some details from the text
- Show some understanding of the dramatic devices used by the writer

The **key words** for recognising a D grade are **some understanding**.

To move from a D to a C you must show the examiner that you can:

- Write a reasonably sustained response
- Understand the dramatic impact of the play
- Support your views thoroughly using details from the play
- Respond personally to the play and its context

The **key words** for recognising a C grade are **relevance** and **analysis**.

Narrating what happens in the play will get you a D grade or lower. Analysing the impact on plot or character or your personal response to events will gain you a C or higher.

For example, imagine the question was **Who do you think is the better leader, Stanhope or Osborne?**

You might write, '**Stanhope is the captain of C Company and Osborne is second in command. Stanhope drinks but is still respected and Osborne is old and wise.**'
This is a straightforward narration of events and character.

Now look at the following:

> **Stanhope is the captain of C Company, but our first impression of him is through Hardy who describes him as 'drinking like a fish'. However, his second in command, Osborne, is loyal to Stanhope and his quick defence of his**

captain shows us that others are loyal to him. Osborne, on the other hand, is quiet and controlled. Hardy describes him as being 'a quiet, sober old thing' and during the play we see how others view him as an approachable character. Both characters show some leadership skills.

This response starts to address the question. It analyses evidence and applies it to the question.

Be selective with your quotations and try to show knowledge of the whole play, so that you can draw links between events.

IMPROVING YOUR RESPONSE TO AN A/A*

To raise your grade to an A/ A* you must show that you:

- Can write responses which are:
  Perceptive
  Original
  Convincing
  Analytical
  Sophisticated

- Have used well selected details

- Have analysed and interpreted the social and historical setting of the play

- Have analysed and interpreted the cultural and literary tradition in which the writer was working

You need to write confidently and use a wide-ranging critical vocabulary.

The **key words** here are **consistent analysis, originality, sophistication** and **confidence**.

If you were aiming for a higher grade, you would need to develop your last response into the following:

Stanhope is the captain of C Company, but our first impression of him is through Hardy who describes him as 'drinking like a fish'. Sherriff cleverly distances us from Stanhope initially, causing us to question his position as leader. However, his second in command, Osborne, is loyal to

EXAMINER'S SECRET
If you discuss the play by considering different interpretations of it and support these with evidence you will get high marks.

Stanhope and quickly defends him, suggesting that he is a man who commands loyalty, despite his flaws. Raleigh's later praise of Stanhope in his letter to Madge reinforces this view of Stanhope as a man worthy of admiration, for even though Raleigh recognises the changes in his old school mate and hero he knows that 'that's because he works so frightfully hard'. We therefore begin to reassess our interpretations of Stanhope. Sherriff presents us with an image of a noble man who has suffered under the strain of war, one of the 'lost generation' of men to whom the play pays homage.

Osborne, on the other hand, is quiet and controlled, typical of his schoolmaster image. Hardy describes him as being 'a quiet, sober old thing' and during the play we see how others view him as an approachable character. He is supportive of Raleigh and Stanhope and is seen talking to various members of C Company. Where Stanhope maintains a strict and disciplined exterior, Osborne, or 'uncle' as he is known, presents himself as open and supportive. Both characters demonstrate facets of leadership.

Here, awareness of Sherriff as a playwright is evident. Instead of just making a comment about a character or incident, you have analysed and interpreted why characters behave as they do – what Sherriff was trying to do with them – and you have linked your comments with the question. You have also referred to various sections of the play showing a thorough and confident knowledge of the text. Your language is also confident and you sound as if you know what you're talking about.

Now, you may be thinking that this all sounds a little bit beyond you, but don't worry. Have a go at planning, preparing, developing and checking your answer and you may find that you know more than you first thought.

SAMPLE ESSAY PLAN

A typical essay question on *Journey's End* is followed by a sample essay plan in note form. This does not present the only answer to the question, merely one answer. Do not be afraid to include your own ideas, and leave out some of those in the sample! Remember that quotations are essential to prove and illustrate the points you make.

> Explore the presentation and importance of Raleigh in the play.

This question requires you to consider two things. It asks you to look at how Sherriff presents Raleigh – in other words what Raleigh is like and how we find this out – and it also asks you to determine what makes him important: how he contributes to the play.

PART 1

Analyse Raleigh's character. He is presented as naïve, romantic, young, inexperienced. Explore how these aspects are made clear to us through stage directions, actions and speech.

PART 2

Examine how Sherriff signals Raleigh's importance – the fact that we meet him early on in the play, before we meet Stanhope – and the fact that the last and most memorable scene is of his death.

PART 3

Explore what function Raleigh serves in the play. Consider his role as a) a commentator on Stanhope, b) as someone who allows greater insights into Stanhope and Osborne, giving the play greater tragic weight, c) as a symbol of the *lost generation*, d) as an example of soldiers who adapted to their environment overcoming barriers of class and e) as a hero and as a foil to other characters.

PART 4

Examine crucial moments where Raleigh's importance is made clear and explore what Sherriff is saying about characters and themes: the letter scene with Stanhope is a dramatically effective moment in the

EXAMINER'S SECRET
Seeing a play in performance is really useful. You can even refer to this in an exam, as long as it's relevant. Discussing a director's particular interpretation of a character would definitely impress the examiner!

play. It makes a critical point about war and provides insight into Osborne, Raleigh and Stanhope. Raleigh's romantic vision of war as expressed in conversation with Osborne is a contrast to Stanhope's cynicism. His death highlights the futility of war; his heroism allows a contrast to Hibbert's cowardice; his changing view of war provides us with an insight into the way in which war forces boys to become men, losing their youth.

Part 5: CONCLUSION

Summarise the lasting impression of Raleigh Sherriff leaves us with and how this suggests his importance in the play.

Further Questions

EXAMINER'S SECRET

Always have all the equipment you need. A spare pen could come in handy!

Make a plan, as shown above, and try these questions:

1. How does Sherriff portray the importance of time in *Journey's End?*

2. Explore the presentation of Trotter and his function in the play.

3. Does Sherriff's presentation of Hibbert encourage you to feel sympathy towards him?

4. In what ways does Osborne's inclusion in the play allow us greater insight into other characters?

5. How does *Journey's End* explore the different ways that men react to war?

6. Sherriff makes Stanhope more attractive as the play develops. To what extent would you agree with this?

7. In what ways do Raleigh's views change during the play?

8. Explore Sherriff's use of humour in the play.

9. Write Osborne's letter to his wife just before he goes on the raid.

10. Write Raleigh's diary entry after the raid and the celebratory dinner.

climax the highest point of tension or drama in a narrative work

colloquialism every day speech

comedy light and humorous drama with a happy ending

comic/ light relief humorous episodes or moments that are inserted in tragic or serious dramas that provide emotional relief from the play's weighty or tragic issues

complication a twist which is introduced into a play to heighten tension and prolong the climax of the story

diction the author's choice of words

dramatic irony a situation where a character is unaware of something the audience knows

explicit clearly expressed

hyperbole a figure of speech in which emphasis is achieved by exaggeration

idiom an expression that does not mean what it literally says

implicit implied, rather than directly expressed

inference implication or impression

irony where the real meaning is concealed or contradicted by the words used

metaphor a figure of speech in which one thing is described as if it were another

mnemonic a way of remembering something based on abbreviation

mood the emotional atmosphere of a scene or moment

personification a figure of speech in which inanimate objects or abstract ideas are given human qualities

simile a comparison between two objects using the words 'like' or 'as'

stage directions advice printed in the text of a play giving instructions to the director and actors regarding movements, gestures, expression and appearance of characters, or on the special effects that are needed at any given moment in the play

symbol/ symbolism an object or image that represents something else

tragedy a work where central characters meet unhappy or disastrous ends, often brought about because of a conflict between characters and higher powers such as law, gods, fate or society

understatement the opposite of hyperbole, understatement is a figure of speech that says less than is intended. It is a form of irony

well made play a type of play popular in the nineteenth and early twentieth century which combined believable incidents and surface realism with a tightly constructed plot

word play witty use of words or punning

CHECKPOINT HINTS/ANSWERS

CHECKPOINT 1
- He is loyal to Stanhope as he defends him, saying he is 'a long way the best company commander' (Act I, p. 4)
- He dislikes others viewing Stanhope as a 'freak show' (Act I, p. 5)
- He knows Stanhope's nerves are battered but he respects him and says he'd 'go to hell with him' (Act I, p. 7)

CHECKPOINT 2
- Osborne is a quiet and calm character who is loyal to his captain. He is middle-aged and obviously close to Stanhope
- Stanhope is twenty-one, has been at the front for three years and has never had a rest. He has a reputation for drinking to excess, but is seen as a good commander

CHECKPOINT 3
- Some mines hit the dugout the previous day
- A German attack is expected and has been expected for about a month
- There's been a lot of movement on the roads and a lot of trains bringing men to the German side, suggesting that their attack is imminent
- The British have 200 yards of front line
- They have two Lewis guns and sentry-posts are marked by crosses on the map
- Trench stores consist of 115 rifle grenades, 500 Mills Bombs and 34 gum boots

CHECKPOINT 4
- He invites him to sit down
- He tells him to take his pack off
- He offers him a drink and cigarette
- He tells him what to call him and advises him to unpack only when he knows where he's sleeping
- He talks to him about Stanhope and life at home

CHECKPOINT 5
- Eating, sleeping, drinking, reading, colouring in circles, smoking, talking about home.

CHECKPOINT 6
- *'He stops short at the sight of Raleigh'* (Act I, p. 18)
- He is described as *'dazed'* (Act I, p. 18)
- He cannot speak and when he does he says, 'How did you get here?' and 'When did you get here?' (Act I, p. 18) suggesting his shock at seeing Raleigh away from home
- He is sarcastic, considering Raleigh's arrival as a coincidence
- He is quiet and irritable, getting angry at Mason over the lack of pepper

CHECKPOINT 7
- He's happy to have apricots and is upset at leaving them to go on duty
- He wants pepper for his soup because war without it is unbearable
- He sips the soup noisily
- He asks what sort of cutlet he is eating
- These instances provide light relief and humour. They also show how Trotter uses food to relieve the strain of war

CHECKPOINT 8
- Stanhope thinks Hibbert is being dishonourable in lying about a condition he does not have, but he has little proof of this and is basing his judgement on instinct. (He is later proved right)

CHECKPOINT 9
- The two of them met when Stanhope spent a summer at Raleigh's family home. He initially saw Madge in the same way he viewed Raleigh as 'another kid' (Act I, p. 28) but then his feelings changed. She is waiting for him and he had hoped to return to her fit and well, but is concerned he may not be able to do so

CHECKPOINT 10
- He threatens to kill Hibbert
- He argues with Hibbert at the celebratory dinner and with Raleigh after the dinner

CHECKPOINT 11
- Trotter says, 'didn't seem a thing in the world alive' (Act II, p. 34)
- Osborne says, 'It's quiet even now' (Act II, p. 34)
- Trotter says, 'Still, I'd rather 'ave a bang or two than this damn quiet' (Act II, p. 36)

CHECKPOINT 12
- Raleigh seems to be nervous and apprehensive, as well as confused. He sits with 'lowered head', is quiet throughout breakfast and only says, 'Yes' in response to Trotter's story about Stanhope's strange behaviour the previous night (Act II, p. 34)

CHECKPOINT 13
- Both can be viewed as sports of a sort. They involve captains and teams of various ranks and positions, as well as strategy and tactics. There is a winning and losing team, a victor and a defeated side

CHECKPOINT 14
- He is making light of his fame and being humorous
- He is suggesting that he is such a celebrity that in order to be spoken to, he requires payment

CHECKPOINT 15
- Stanhope's response to food, 'So I gather' (Act II, p. 40) and 'I should loathe it' (Act II, p. 41)
- Osborne's remark about his sons playing toy soldiers, 'I wish I knew how to fight a battle like those boys of mine' (Act II, p. 44)

CHECKPOINT 16
- Worms are found in dirt and earth and this is where they may soon end up, dead, eaten by worms. The worms' lack of direction is a parallel with their own feelings of hopelessness

CHECKPOINT 17
- His reasons are personal rather than professional, so whilst he has the right, as captain, to censor letters he is unfair in singling out Raleigh for this treatment

CHECKPOINT 18
- His embarrassment and laughter
- His desire to not send the letter after all
- His reluctance to hand it over

CHECKPOINT 19
- He 'sits with his head in his hand, digging a magazine with a pencil' (Act II, p. 47)

CHECKPOINT 20
- Left – Stanhope and Sergeant Baker, platoons number eleven and twelve
- Right – Osborne and the sergeant major, platoons number nine and ten

CHECKPOINT 21
- To find out who has come into the enemy line in preparation for the attack

CHECKPOINT 22
- Pauses, silences, our knowledge of Stanhope's views of Hibbert and Stanhope's emotional state, Stanhope looking silently at Hibbert and later undoing his revolver holster, threat of death, the countdown of seconds, the emotional outbursts and exclamations

CHECKPOINT 23
- A guiding tape will be laid and holes made in the German and British wires to secure a passage for the men

CHECKPOINT 24
- He suggests that Stanhope rests but Stanhope says there's too much work to be done. We know he has told Hibbert he will accompany him on his duty

CHECKPOINT 25
- Trotter remarks on Hibbert's eyes. He thinks he's been crying and calls him a 'funny little bloke' (Act II, p. 65)

CHECKPOINT 26
- He talks about an 'empty feeling inside' (Act III, p. 71)

CHECKPOINT 27
- He asks which town the boy was born in rather than which town he has come from

CHECKPOINT 28
- Uncertain: he has said he will try to stick it out, but he shows a rather unsavoury side to his character when he shows everyone his pictures of women at the dinner

CHECKPOINT 29
- He says, 'You've 'ad too much champagne you 'ave' (Act III, p. 82) and looks at him in a sinister way

CHECKPOINT 30
- He is sad at Osborne's death and knows the attack will come soon. He has lost his best friend and fears he may lose others too, including Raleigh, and there is nothing he can do to stop things from happening

CHECKPOINT 31
- The gunfire sounds like a dissatisfied person – a symbol of the enemy, but also of war itself, an attack that has been kept waiting for too long

CHECKPOINT 32
- Stanhope had suggested the previous night that Trotter was unemotional and never felt like he was so happy he wanted to sing, and here he is singing
- His song is about a long trail winding; perhaps he is referring to the uncertain path towards death

CHECKPOINT 33
- Raleigh is lain on Osborne's bed, the same one Stanhope told him to get off after Osborne's death. Stanhope clearly views Raleigh as his best friend now and recognises the imminence of his death

CHECKPOINT 34
- Stanhope bathes Raleigh's face with water
- He tells him to lie still
- He promises that he will get him taken away to the dressing station and hospital
- He tells him his legs are just numb from the shock of the injury, and that he's not to blame
- He gets him some water and finally brings him a candle for light

CHECKPOINT 35
- Sad because of Raleigh's death but also tense because of the personified anger of the attack outside which is waiting to claim the lives of the remaining men. There is a stillness and emptiness at the end of the scene like the cold and dark of death to which Raleigh refers. We recognise the futility of it all

TEST YOURSELF (ACT I)

1 Raleigh
2 Mason
3 Trotter
4 Osborne
5 Osborne
6 Stanhope
7 Hibbert
8 Raleigh

TEST YOURSELF (ACT II)

1 Osborne
2 Stanhope
3 Raleigh
4 Hibbert
5 Stanhope
6 Raleigh
7 Hibbert
8 Osborne and Raleigh

TEST YOURSELF (ACT III)

1 Osborne
2 Raleigh
3 Hibbert
4 Stanhope
5 Osborne and Raleigh
6 Trotter
7 Osborne
8 Raleigh

NOTES

NOTES

Maya Angelou
I Know Why the Caged Bird Sings

Jane Austen
Pride and Prejudice

Alan Ayckbourn
Absent Friends

Elizabeth Barrett Browning
Selected Poems

Robert Bolt
A Man for All Seasons

Harold Brighouse
Hobson's Choice

Charlotte Brontë
Jane Eyre

Emily Brontë
Wuthering Heights

Brian Clark
Whose Life is it Anyway?

Robert Cormier
Heroes

Shelagh Delaney
A Taste of Honey

Charles Dickens
David Copperfield
Great Expectations
Hard Times
Oliver Twist
Selected Stories

Roddy Doyle
Paddy Clarke Ha Ha Ha

George Eliot
Silas Marner
The Mill on the Floss

Anne Frank
The Diary of a Young Girl

William Golding
Lord of the Flies

Oliver Goldsmith
She Stoops to Conquer

Willis Hall
The Long and the Short and the Tall

Thomas Hardy
Far from the Madding Crowd
The Mayor of Casterbridge
Tess of the d'Urbervilles
The Withered Arm and other Wessex Tales

L. P. Hartley
The Go-Between

Seamus Heaney
Selected Poems

Susan Hill
I'm the King of the Castle

Barry Hines
A Kestrel for a Knave

Louise Lawrence
Children of the Dust

Harper Lee
To Kill a Mockingbird

Laurie Lee
Cider with Rosie

Arthur Miller
The Crucible
A View from the Bridge

Robert O'Brien
Z for Zachariah

Frank O'Connor
My Oedipus Complex and Other Stories

George Orwell
Animal Farm

J. B. Priestley
An Inspector Calls
When We Are Married

Willy Russell
Educating Rita
Our Day Out

J. D. Salinger
The Catcher in the Rye

William Shakespeare
Henry IV Part I
Henry V
Julius Caesar
Macbeth
The Merchant of Venice
A Midsummer Night's Dream
Much Ado About Nothing
Romeo and Juliet
The Tempest
Twelfth Night

George Bernard Shaw
Pygmalion

Mary Shelley
Frankenstein

R. C. Sherriff
Journey's End

Rukshana Smith
Salt on the snow

John Steinbeck
Of Mice and Men

Robert Louis Stevenson
Dr Jekyll and Mr Hyde

Jonathan Swift
Gulliver's Travels

Robert Swindells
Daz 4 Zoe

Mildred D. Taylor
Roll of Thunder, Hear My Cry

Mark Twain
Huckleberry Finn

James Watson
Talking in Whispers

Edith Wharton
Ethan Frome

William Wordsworth
Selected Poems

A Choice of Poets

Mystery Stories of the Nineteenth Century including The Signalman

Nineteenth Century Short Stories

Poetry of the First World War

Six Women Poets

For the AQA Anthology:

Duffy and Armitage & Pre-1914 Poetry

Heaney and Clarke & Pre-1914 Poetry

Poems from Different Cultures

Margaret Atwood
Cat's Eye
The Handmaid's Tale

Jane Austen
Emma
Mansfield Park
Persuasion
Pride and Prejudice
Sense and Sensibility

William Blake
Songs of Innocence and of Experience

Charlotte Brontë
Jane Eyre
Villette

Emily Brontë
Wuthering Heights

Angela Carter
Nights at the Circus
Wise Children

Geoffrey Chaucer
The Franklin's Prologue and Tale
The Merchant's Prologue and Tale
The Miller's Prologue and Tale
The Prologue to the Canterbury Tales
The Wife of Bath's Prologue and Tale

Samuel Coleridge
Selected Poems

Joseph Conrad
Heart of Darkness

Daniel Defoe
Moll Flanders

Charles Dickens
Bleak House
Great Expectations
Hard Times

Emily Dickinson
Selected Poems

John Donne
Selected Poems

Carol Ann Duffy
Selected Poems

George Eliot
Middlemarch
The Mill on the Floss

T. S. Eliot
Selected Poems
The Waste Land

F. Scott Fitzgerald
The Great Gatsby

E. M. Forster
A Passage to India

Charles Frazier
Cold Mountain

Brian Friel
Making History
Translations

William Golding
The Spire

Thomas Hardy
Jude the Obscure
The Mayor of Casterbridge
The Return of the Native
Selected Poems
Tess of the d'Urbervilles

Seamus Heaney
Selected Poems from 'Opened Ground'

Nathaniel Hawthorne
The Scarlet Letter

Homer
The Iliad
The Odyssey

Aldous Huxley
Brave New World

Kazuo Ishiguro
The Remains of the Day

Ben Jonson
The Alchemist

James Joyce
Dubliners

John Keats
Selected Poems

Philip Larkin
The Whitsun Weddings and Selected Poems

Ian McEwan
Atonement

Christopher Marlowe
Doctor Faustus
Edward II

Arthur Miller
Death of a Salesman

John Milton
Paradise Lost Books I & II

Toni Morrison
Beloved

George Orwell
Nineteen Eighty-Four

Sylvia Plath
Selected Poems

Alexander Pope
Rape of the Lock & Selected Poems

William Shakespeare
Antony and Cleopatra
As You Like It
Hamlet
Henry IV Part I
King Lear
Macbeth
Measure for Measure
The Merchant of Venice
A Midsummer Night's Dream
Much Ado About Nothing
Othello
Richard II
Richard III
Romeo and Juliet
The Taming of the Shrew
The Tempest
Twelfth Night
The Winter's Tale

George Bernard Shaw
Saint Joan

Mary Shelley
Frankenstein

Bram Stoker
Dracula

Jonathan Swift
Gulliver's Travels and A Modest Proposal

Alfred Tennyson
Selected Poems

Alice Walker
The Color Purple

Oscar Wilde
The Importance of Being Earnest

Tennessee Williams
A Streetcar Named Desire
The Glass Menagerie

Jeanette Winterson
Oranges Are Not the Only Fruit

John Webster
The Duchess of Malfi

Virginia Woolf
To the Lighthouse

William Wordsworth
The Prelude and Selected Poems

W. B. Yeats
Selected Poems

Metaphysical Poets